PROPERTY INVESTING MADE SIMPLE

7 Tips to Reducing Property Investment Risk
and Creating Real Wealth

ANDREW CROSSLEY

First published in 2014
This edition published February 2014

ISBN-13: 978-0-9924325-9-1

Copyright © 2014 Andrew Crossley

Edited and Published by Busybird Publishing
Printed and bound in Australia by McPherson's Printing Group
Cover image: Kev Howlett
Cover design Busybird Publishing
Layout and typesetting: Chameleon Print Design
Typeset in Minion Pro and Glober

Busybird Publishing
PO Box 855
Eltham Victoria
Australia 3095

*'Whenever you find yourself on the side of the majority,
it is time to pause and reflect.'*
— Mark Twain

Remember this if you're tempted to join the crowd of buyers succumbing to the tactics of property marketing companies, spruikers, and anyone else representing the seller.

Disclaimer

The content of this book — including its strategies, ideas, concepts, explanations, definitions and opinions — do not constitute advice. After all, everyone's personal situation is different and expert advice must be sought in each case. You will realise that this book has not taken into account your personal situation, goals, attempts at fact finding, your risk profile and a multitude of other factors. This book is for education purposes. Risks are involved with all investments, so you must seek appropriate advice before making any decision, we disclaim all liability for any decision you may choose to make.

I have taken every reasonable effort to ensure the accuracy of the contents in this book. Neither I nor anyone involved in this book, in any manner whatsoever, accepts any responsibility for any action/purchase that you take as a result of the motivation that you will hopefully receive from the contents of this book.

Obtain expert advice before you implement anything.

Dedication

I dedicate this book to my wife Els and to my children, Ben and Lisa.
You can achieve anything in life. Dream big.
No one has the right to stand in your way.

Acknowledgements

Writing a book is an exciting journey.

I would like to thank the many people who have contributed, and who have also helped make it an enjoyable experience:

Coral Page (Knox Taxation) — for her encouraging words, her great personality and the contribution to the accounting information included. What a great team we make in co-ordinating seminars.

Garry Harvey ('The Property Guy') — for the enormous value he added to my journey and my book, for his encouragement and for his friendship. You are a legend, Garry.

Pearl Yeo and Athol Park (Centre for Transformation) — who run workshops entitled 'Journey for Transformation', and help many address and overcome fear: the biggest hurdle for most people. My good friends.

Ian Donaldson (All Purpose Property Inspections) — for your contribution and time.

Vivienne Weston and Stacey Cox (Ray White Frankston) — for providing valuable insights on property management and for being one of my property managers.

John Couroyannis CPA, FIPA, ASIC Registered SMSF Auditor, J.C. Accounting Services — for his insights.

PIAA — Parts of the material in this book are derived from and/ or interpreted from material provided in The Property Investment

Association of Australia's Property Investment Advice Course (PIA01) and reference to Forrester Cohen Services. I would like to thank John Moore and Rosemary Johnston for their mentoring, support, ongoing commitment, and friendship. Their insights have been invaluable.

Andrew Larcombe and Vanessa Lewis from Morbanx — for being my go-to brokers in providing solutions to my own lending requirements.

Jenny Newman, 21 Century Unlimited — for her time in being interviewed.

Joseph Rose (Rose Lawyers) — for his time in being interviewed and Joseph's office for assisting with the disclaimer.

Andrew Burgan (Lime Financial) — for his time in being interviewed.

Blaise van Hecke of Busybird Publishing — for editing, cover design and publishing. An absolute pleasure to work with.

Special thanks to my father, Tony Crossley — for his valuable contributions following his forty years in the real estate industry. Also, my Mum and sister for their wisdom.

Finally, the biggest thanks and appreciation must go to my wonderful wife Els, and our beautiful children, Ben and Lisa. They have gone above and beyond with their support and patience.

Contents

Preface   Consider Your Current Reality 1

About this Book 5

About the Author 7

Chapter 1   Overcoming the Fear Factor 11

Chapter 2   Shady Advice versus the Right Advice 19

Chapter 3   Buying the Right Property 33

Chapter 4   Wise Choice/choose wisely 45

Chapter 5   Choosing the right Strategies 67

Chapter 6   Game Plan 89

Chapter 7   Best Property Management 115

Chapter 8   Money Talks 129

Chapter 9   Accounting "The Money" 153

Chapter 10   Financial Freedom 175

Team Working for YOU ... BONUS TIP 191

Insurances 195

Summary 197

Contact Me 201

Glossary 203

Resources 205

Preface

Consider Your Current Reality

If you think too long or don't act with property investment, you could end up being one of the 99% of the population retiring on less than $40k per annum. Fear and uncertainty are the major drivers of procrastination. Often, when someone does make an effort by haphazardly researching, it can lead to analysis paralysis, and nothing ever happens.

Negative gearing, as a strategy, has been oversold. Too many people have been burnt by *overly* negative gearing, e.g. purchasing a property that is too negatively geared for their lifestyle, or by purchasing too many negatively geared properties that absorb surplus cash flow.

There is no guarantee as to when property prices will rise, or rather, rise in the short term. Over the long term, however, property prices **do** rise — yet many people get caught in the moment like a deer in headlights and they put off purchasing, telling themselves it's not the right time to buy. If you hold onto property, in the long term, it will compensate for the fact that no one is clever enough to pick when the exact and right time to buy property is.

- The standard of superannuation returns over the last decade was below 6% (ABC Investigation, Sydney Morning Herald, 5 August 2010)
- 86% of Australians will retire on an income of just $16k (Canberra University Research, 2010)
- 72% of all property investors only own one property (ATO, 2010)

How you can increase your wealth

Most people don't succeed in property investment for many reasons. The main reason is that they don't seek the right advice or right help — **independent help** (and specifically independent to the property provider, location and selection).

Other significant considerations, that the right advice can address and help you with, are:

1. Help with your choice of conveyancing services
2. Involving a quantity surveyor
3. Help to locate a reliable property manager
4. Discuss purchasing entities, i.e. a trust, or have it under your own name
5. Help you locate a good accountant
6. Locating a good broker. Loan structure is very important
7. Modelling of holding costs — taking into account interest, rates, insurance, possible maintenance, agent's fees, body corporate, and other holding costs versus income from the property.

You could go to a property marketing company engaged by a developer to sell their stock, but:

*   they typically represent the seller, and unethically pretend to represent the buyer in the same transaction
*   the client is limited to the properties the marketing firm is engaged to sell
*   you will probably be told that any property the marketing company has to sell, in your price range, is suitable for you. This is wrong!
*   the client's needs should lead the choice of property. The property should not lead the client.

Most people understand they should invest toward their future, but unfortunately, they seem to think their superannuation will do it for them, or they just wait for things to happen. Waiting and procrastinating can be your downfall.

As an investor, have you ever faced the following challenges?

Been overwhelmed by the number of choices in the property market? Do you particularly know where to buy, what property, and at what time, to have the greatest positive impact on your wealth creation?

Are you able to tell the genuine advisors from the ones who have hidden agendas, or who masquerade around as a so-called 'advisor'?

Do you wonder who receives remuneration in your property transaction — and how much?

Is your advisor really acting in your best interests, or are they a real estate agent, or property marketing company, employed (and paid directly) by the vendor to move their property?

Is your advisor professionally accredited and qualified to provide you with good advice?

Do you know what style of property may, or may not, be allowable for your SMSF — your Self-Managed Super Fund?

And the list goes on, and it all adds to the property puzzle!

Becoming wealthy is a process and it takes discipline. You need to follow proven strategies and take action, and it's never too late to start. No matter what your age or current circumstances, consider making a decision to start investing today.

About this Book

Many books out there are designed to sell a specific strategy or style of property wanting you to believe it is the best for the investor. The reality is there are many styles of property and many strategies that suit some people and not others. Often when different strategies are combined, it improves your portfolio and reduces your risk by spreading out how exposed you are to just one or two variations. It is necessary for investors to understand this point as it will prove important when starting or continuing to build a portfolio.

Upon the completion of reading this book, you will have a much better understanding of the importance of having a strategy to avoid following the herd. You will know more about ownership structures, lending requirements/considerations, and, most importantly, avoiding property spruikers and companies that represent the seller — not the buyer. Everyone needs a team or people around them as none of us know everything. I will highlight who you must have in your team for success.

Most people have a pain or problem they need to address and overcome. The problem could be not knowing how to reduce risk, lesson impact on your lifestyle when investing in property, successfully build a portfolio, knowing where to go for advice and how to overcome fear. This book will provide you answers to overcoming these problems.

Property investment is a journey of strategy, but not just any strategy.

This book is designed to educate the majority of investors, who are time-poor and may be disillusioned with the share market. It is for those who recognise the importance of doing something positive in order to have a more prosperous future in retirement.

People often listen to those who have an uneducated opinion, developed through little experience or hearsay, with limited knowledge or fact. Think about this quote:

> *'If you go to work on your goals, your goals will go to work on you.*
> *If you go to work on your plan, your plan will go to work on you.*
> *Whatever good things we build, end up building us.'*
> **— Jim Rohn**

About the Author

Growing up in Melbourne, Andrew Crossley left Australia at a young age and soon began working in London for an advertising and marketing firm, which led to landing a role at a prestigious investment firm dealing with share market investors. In 1996, at the age of twenty-four, Andrew was headhunted and moved to Rotterdam to work for a private equity firm. For eight years he dealt with high net-worth clients, handling investments in venture capital projects, international property funds, IPOs and off-market derivatives.

A company move to the Cayman Islands resulted in Andrew selling his 'off the plan' purchased apartment. He made the mistake of purchasing it off someone else who had bought it from the developer. The individual bought it prospectively, before it was built, then on-sold it to Andrew before it was completed. Consequently, Andrew learnt, from experience, that what someone presents to you as a viable property investment is not necessarily the case!

Fortunately, the two-bedroom apartment in the heart of Rotterdam, which came with a separate car park and storage room, proved a success. After three years, he sold the apartment for a 50% profit, and had the foresight to separate and sell the car space individually. He made further profit of $40k as a result. Hence, the entrepreneur in Andrew was born.

Having married Els and arriving back in Australia in 2005, Andrew became a front-person for several recruitment companies in Melbourne, many of whom he believes often prejudice expats and new residents. One common theme emerged: his overseas qualifications and experience didn't particularly count in Australia. Disappointing: yes; a deterrent to success: no!

Andrew began to look at Australian governmental policy and realised that longer-living Australians were destined to suffer, longer term, unless they seriously looked at how they could self-fund their living standards in retirement. He realised he had to have a plan.

Andrew set about finding a path to financial security through property — for himself and his family, and to secure an early retirement. He realised the onus was on him. Choosing to do nothing proactive would mean a life on the pension, whatever that amount of payment might end up being.

Andrew drew strength from completing three Masters Degrees — an MBA, a Masters of Commerce, and Masters of Commercial Law. He became a qualified financial planner, mortgage broker, estate agent (in Victoria and N.S.W.), and then became a qualified property advisor. Formulating a property investment business plan was a natural progression, completed by making use of financial modelling tools, a personal and enduring code of ethics, and decision-making criteria.

Andrew became employed by the largest non-bank in Australia, based on funds under management, and gained further experience with the largest, publicly-listed mortgage manager in Australia, Homeloans Ltd. Andrew was also a finalist in the Mortgage and Finance Association of Australia 'business development manager of the year' awards. Working with others who think outside the box, he understood how credit assessors work, and how lending policy can work for and against an investor.

Now owning ten properties, his rental income is well on the way to replacing his normal income. The strategy, now, is to see that his rental income provides an excellent lifestyle in the next fifteen years.

His clients can benefit from his well-structured planning skills, underpinned by a sound risk management strategy, to find financial security.

Andrew's invaluable understanding of the economic and tax framework of property, in addition to the overall framework of investing in property and growing wealth through property investment, culminated in a prestigious award from the Australian 'Your Investment Property Magazine' Property Investor Awards 2012.

> *'If you have knowledge, let others light their candles with it.'*
> **— Winston Churchill**

Andrew Crossley — Personal Motivation Statement

It's all about YOU!

Far too often I see people being burned by sales companies, marketing companies and individuals recognised as 'spruikers'. Let's not confuse spruikers with reputable real estate companies, who are often honest about whom they act for; most (if not all) of the time, it is the seller, or vendor, that they represent.

I must say, I have dealt with many property marketing companies, and not all are bad. There are a very small handful (okay maybe a handful around the country) who try to do the right thing, such as disclose commissions, ensure those commissions are fair — with no bonuses being paid — and whose valuations stack up.

People know they need to take action to invest wisely in property, on the whole, but don't know where to go. Or, they have tried and failed in the property investment market because **they didn't seek the right advice**.

I believe it is my purpose to help *and* educate people.

I enjoy sharing my knowledge and helping others. Community giving, such as being a member of Lions' Club International and serving as a Justice of the Peace, afford me the opportunity to give back. 'Givers get' is what I believe.

Happy Reading,
Andrew Crossley

'If a man empties his purse into his head, no man can take it away from him. An investment in knowledge always pays the best interest.'
— Benjamin Franklin

Chapter 1

Overcoming the Fear Factor

Fear

'Fear directs people. True learning comes from passion, energy and desire. When it comes to money, people play it safe to feel secure. Passion does not direct them. The main cause of financial struggle is fear and ignorance.'
— **Robert Kiyosaki**

My advice is to avoid the naysayers, the people who talk negatively about property. If you listen to them, they will always have a theory about a property bubble, about interest rates shooting up, or they simply want things that are just not possible (such as a guaranteed this or guaranteed that.) The naysayers don't take responsibility for themselves. They have never left the playground, and are most likely failures in their investment life. They favour excuses over results and effort.

Often these people feel lonely in their failures in life and want to pull you down that slippery slope, to justify or reinforce their own lack of success, lack of action, or state of not being in-motion.

Maybe the reason people choose to avoid uncertainty and therefore (by default) they choose a future of poverty, rather than being in-motion by thinking proactively about their future, is that poverty is a reliable and certain outcome, and the other is more uncomfortable because it is unknown. Living in the present seems to be more important than living for the future, in balance with living for the present, therefore, by the time they get to the future it's too late.

Some people believe there is a perfect property out there, and unless they find it they don't do anything. All those 'what ifs' play on people's minds. What if I can't get a tenant? What if, when I do get a tenant, they cause damage? What if it floods? What if I make a mistake? What if the advice or information is wrong? What if there is something better, or rates change, or I see something better next week, or my friends think I'm mad?

There are answers to most of these things, but the procrastinators, the people suffering from inaction and fear and 'future damaging' so-called priorities, will dream up new 'what ifs' and, eventually, it can become very difficult (or impossible) to remain connected with common sense, perspective, reality and/or rational thought. To lots of people fear of doing something is more debilitating than the fear of **not** doing something.

Common Excuses or things that get in the way

Age Related Issues:
Under 30 years

- Too young.
- Spending money and going out is more of a priority than thinking about investing.
- Wedding expenses may be a factor.
- Buying a first home or considering having children.

Between 30–50 years
- School fees.

- Holidays.
- Bills.
- Pressures, or fear of instability, at work.

Between 50–60 years

- School and university fees.
- Stock market and superannuation suffering leaving a sour taste and fear.
- Despondency, and feeling like it is too late.

60+ years

- Hard to get a loan without an exit strategy.
- Feeling life is financially over, and what could have been 'green grass heading out to pasture' is now barren and drought ridden turf.

The Fear Factor itself

The sooner people face their fear, the sooner they can start to work on it, address it, confront it, and work to overcome it, to accept it whilst being able to take action and get into motion. The sooner we discover the problem, the sooner we can try to fix it, or look for a solution.

Every person, when it comes to investing, has one of two things in common: either they have lots of excuses, or they have results. Results come from action. Excuses are a result of inaction and lead to inaction. Often it's 'the chicken or the egg' scenario that leads to failure in retirement. Failure is ending up on the pension. Results come from action. They provide the opportunity for a future, and investing toward the future gives you opportunity. It gives you hope.

The Scared Factor

- No tenant.
- Interest rate movement.
- Job loss.
- Bank won't lend.
- Complexities of managing the property.

Retirement

With the number of baby boomers retiring in the next few years, I am concerned for both them and also for the next retiring generation. Will the Government have the money to fund all of our retirements, given that the majority of people end up on the pension due to failure to create wealth in their lives, which would provide for a passive income in retirement?

As there will be fewer people in the work force, and with humans living longer, the Government will gather less tax and will, likely, be forced to review the pension eligibility. They may then continue to restrict voluntary contributions into superannuation just as they have done before.

It's a shame that people don't have as much fear of merely 'existing' in retirement, rather than 'living life' in retirement, as they should. Merely 'existing' is when someone lives off a pension and has little money to do anything more significant than the occasional caravan park holiday, bingo outing, or crossword day with friends. If the fear of the 'financially-poor future', which most people end up in, was stronger than the 'fear of doing something' then more people would take action, and seek out the right advice. Ultimately fear is illogical, based on something that *might* happen, but may *never* happen.

Some people use the excuse that money is not important in life. They conveniently forget how much good can be done, and how many charities could benefit, if those people had money to give away. These are probably the same people who go to a church and cite religion as a reason why money is not important — that same church that passes a bowl around asking for money. Obviously, the church sees the importance and value of money, and the good that can be achieved with it.

Analysis Paralysis

Buying property involves risk. Undertaking research is necessary and unavoidable. Many people who undertake research get trapped in the detail though, or they simply keep looking and never find what they think they should find. Most investors do not understand the research data they are reading either, which is another reason why there are currently only approximately 14,000 Australians who have six properties or more (according to the ATO.)

If you seek assistance and guidance advice, you can alleviate many of the concerns you have, as it is concerns (and indeed self-talk excuses) that prevent you from moving forward: thinking you must get more information, and second guessing yourself that you don't have enough. Accepting the fact that mistakes will happen can help, and the size of the mistake can be reduced by conducting good research.

No one is perfect at timing the property market in every location. Even in a single chosen location it is difficult to perfectly time entering the market, but you must understand that by holding the property long enough, you can mitigate these errors in timing. Naturally, it is important to reduce the risk of getting the timing 'massively wrong' versus 'a little bit'.

Not knowing where to go for help in the Property Industry

Property spruikers are everywhere in the property industry.

What is a spruiker? Austral archaic slang to speak in public, used esp. of a showman or salesman (http://www.thefreedictionary.com). They are likened to a touter: 'touting occurs when a person advertises, promotes, or otherwise describes a security for sale without disclosing that the person is being paid to do so' (Wikipedia).

According to http://www.allwords.com, two definitions are provided:

1. (*Australian*) One who promotes his own cause; one who toots their own horn.
2. (*figurative*) A person standing outside a place of business trying to persuade patrons to enter, or vigorously trying to persuade customers to purchase their wares.

Property is currently an unregulated industry thus allowing all manner of operators to freely function. The most typical sign of a spruiker is an operator who runs evening seminars. They have their cronies/assistants standing in the corners, somewhat camouflaged, then out of nowhere towards the end of the presentation, they appear — a bit like sales agents at an auction, but less ethical. These people talk about how many people don't own properties, and the gloom and doom of people retiring with nothing. This is all true, but, the problem is they take advantage and pounce on this reality with properties they conveniently have for sale, which, conveniently, will suit all people that fit the basic requirement: often a $60k income, and a pulse.

I met a spruiker recently. He was the typical type: young, with a smooth sales pitch. This guy was about twenty-five and represented another known property spruiker, selling land-banking options.

The sales pitch was pay $3000 now and secure a property worth $400k in five years' time in a large development of several thousand houses — a master plan estate. These planned communities are huge developments with shopping centres, gyms, social activity centres, etc. The problem was that this particular spruiker was arguably (albeit possibly unintentionally) misleading the audience.

When I sat down with this young guy later, he mentioned figures of $16–18k deposit, rather than $3k. People are basically being enticed into these projects on the back of paying a deposit now to secure the rights to future production. More naïve investors present probably purchased two or three of these investment properties, without considering that, in five years' time, they would have to acquire finance of $1.2million (based on the price being promoted, unless they could on-sell the rights to the contract). It could be a lose/lose for some people, as either the properties will not be worth what they are being promoted they *could* be worth, or they have potentially over-committed. Who knows what they will be earning in five years, or if they will even be in a realistic position to settle as per the contract? Who knows what these developments will actually be worth, when there are literally thousands of these things being built?

The other problem, besides the presenter misleading people, and their clients succumbing to buying one (or many) of these things, is the sales guy himself. He stated to me that he had 'been in property all his life'. Who at the age of around twenty-five would have the knowledge, experience, and wisdom to be an expert? It's laughable. I also asked him what his opinion was of NRAS (National Rental Affordability Scheme), just to test his knowledge. Many people haven't heard of the strategy/scheme but someone in property 'all their life' should know. He didn't! I had to explain it to him.

Funny thing is he did continue trying to sell to me, albeit less energetically, after I informed him of how many properties I owned. He kept going, a bit like a greyhound chasing a rabbit. He just didn't have the wisdom to know when to stop and move on.

Relevant experience and qualifications help sift through the salespeople out there, and getting to the true property advisors. They should possess not just experience, and not just education. They must have both. I personally would never use a financial planner who had not invested in any of the managed funds he was recommending. Likewise, a true property advisor must be insured to provide advice. They must have suitable qualifications as well, and they must have personal experience in purchasing property, some of which is found in the areas he or she is sourcing.

Advisors, in my opinion, must have a qualification for being a property investment advisor.

'Often the difference between a successful man and a failure is not one's better abilities or ideas, but the courage that one has to bet on his ideas, to take a calculated risk — and to act.'
— Maxwell Maltz

Chapter 2

Shady Advice versus the Right Advice ... TIP 1

'Know-how will surpass guess-how.'
— Unknown

Not financial advisors

Many people, when they think of obtaining advice, turn to financial planners/financial advisors. Let's bust the myth that they can help you with specific property research and property sourcing.

The financial planning industry deals with investment products (securities). Currently, the Australian Securities and Exchange Commission — ASIC — does not recognise property as an investment security, although, more recently (as of late 2013), property in an SMSF (self-managed super fund) is a financial product.

ASIC (an independent Commonwealth Government body) contribute to the wellbeing and reputation of the Australian economy, helping investors become more informed and confident by ensuring fairness and transparency in Australia's financial markets. Their responsibility includes enforcing and giving effect to the law, making information available to the public on companies and other bodies.

Generally, financial advisor licensing requirements do not permit them to provide specific property advice, or provide product. A good financial planner will generally provide advice on asset allocation of funds, of which a proportion may be allocated to property.

Shares, managed funds, superannuation structures and insurance are predominately the main examples of what ASIC regulates and what financial planners may be able to advise on. It does not typically include specific property, nor does it include credit advice like mortgages.

The bigger issue for advisors is they have not traditionally been able to obtain professional indemnity insurance, to advise on specific property. They need to advise on it as an *asset class* but, under their financial planning licence, they cannot typically provide specific advice on specific property. At the time of writing this, there are only two education firms in Australia that have attained professional indemnity insurance for property advice.

Most financial advisors work for institutions, and they are often governing what *their* advisors offer you, by way of the product they recommend. They conveniently (and typically) recommend their own institutionally-owned products. A bit like a bank, they may only offer you their own products. This may severely limit both you and what you actually need.

Some financial planners give the industry a bad name. They receive kickbacks from developers by passing their client over to buy a property. These are often, if not always, undisclosed. We are talking about amounts of 2%+, plus additional incentives (such as an extra 1%, or bonuses) for certain projects.

Unlike regulated industries such as accounting and financial planning, working for a property marketing company (as distinct from operating as a traditional real estate agent), does not require a great deal of education, experience, or study prowess. Marketing investment property, put simply, requires nothing really but the ability to sell, and this *is* meant to be a wake-up call and warning!

Literally anyone can be involved in property, which has resulted in there being many predators in the field. The property market has also attracted highly ethical people, and they are very professional. With so much noise and distraction everywhere, it is (all too often) difficult to spot the difference between the good and the bad.

There is no representative body to which the ethical property professionals can belong.

There are really only two organisations that are trying to lead change in the industry. However, at the time of writing, there is only one organisation's training syllabus — that being PIAA (Property Investment Association of Australia) — that is recognised as adequately suitable, in the insurer's eyes, for their advisors to be eligible for professional indemnity insurance. PI insurance is reasonably easy to obtain in some industries as simple sometimes as just buying it, if you have a small amount of money and some basics in place. Why having PI insurance is so different in the property industry and why it is so very important to only deal with someone that has it is because you cannot simply buy it off the rack as it were. There really is only one model of operation to which we must adhere, to be eligible and entitled to receive it.

The quality of their structure and information provides property advisors with the framework that addresses several key points (which any regulated industry requires), and in my opinion and experience, this sets the benchmark as to what is required for the property industry to become regulated.

The fundamental backbone of any regulated industry should follow these key points:

- Barrier of Entry — Advisors must complete the PIAA Property Advisor Course, complete either a NSW Agents' Representative Course, or the full course, to obtain a full license as a real estate agent (equivalent to what is required to work as a real estate agent.)
- Adherence to a code of conduct, and commitment to appropriate transparency of any vested interest, commissions, or conflicts of interest
- Provision of professional indemnity insurance
- See that complaints procedures are managed by members
- Inclusion of a model designed to encourage and allow industry participation, and develop greater levels of professionalism (rather than a model designed simply to enforce compliance.)

'It meets a number of issues raised by the Consumer Protection Laws and also by the Joint Parliamentary Committee.'
— PIAA

Participants of the Property Investment Association of Australia Course must also have attained RG146, otherwise known as the Diploma in Financial Services (Financial Planning). This makes them qualified as a financial planner as well.

All of this acquired knowledge culminates in an individual who has the adequate education to allow the professional indemnity insurance provider to then provide them with cover. The fact that a person is eligible for professional indemnity insurance sets them apart from everyone else. Those in the industry who are not eligible to receive property indemnity insurance should not, and must not, provide property advice. Alas, it is not that simple. This insurance is not something you can just buy like some other industries can as already mentioned. You have to earn it and be entitled to it, and be considered a reasonable enough risk, i.e. low risk. Most property marketing operators are not considered to be a reasonably low, acceptable, or trustworthy risk. They, therefore, can usually only apply for insurance to sell property, but not provide advice on it based on how their model generally works, (many should not even be allowed to have this type of insurance in my opinion)

Many people masquerade as property advisors, but many are little more than smooth, simple and single-minded sales people.

'Investors are currently left without sufficient education about the quality of the support they have access to':

- There is no Yellow Pages listing for Property Investment Advisors with professional accreditation, and no recognised standard.
- Websites offering 'advice' services have no identifiable reference to business or professional standards.
- The media supports the popular misconception that the number of properties in your portfolio is the measure of a good educator, consultant or advisor, based on the premise if they have done it so can I. This offers no tailoring to a client's current circumstances, their risk profile and appetite, or their targeted outcome(s).
- Add to this that property is an unregulated investment asset class. As a result, there are no standards for the style of claims that can be made. Many claims come from the puffery and emotional manipulation of the real estate home ownership market, some from the multi-thousand 'secrets of investing' seminars, and a few from the Advice Professionals acting in the client's best interests.'
  — PIAA

PIAA's high standards act as a barrier of entry into property advice. A barrier to entry refers to educational, ethical and administrative requirements, which are often viewed as too cumbersome or unnecessary for spruikers to want to adhere to, hence the problem in the industry. A reminder to you that most people in the property industry are not appropriately qualified as financial planners in conjunction with being buyer's agents/ real estate agents and in conjunction with being property advisors and thus are not eligible to be a member, and are not eligible for insurance to provide advice. Many operators do not want to undertake these requirements anyway as they have become used to making huge commissions by having relationships with the developers (sellers/vendors).

'The Safe as Houses Report post Henry Kaye and other spruikers, published in June 2005, identified a number of key requirements to attract Government regulation. PIAA has used this as a standard for many years. More recently, the regulation of mortgage professionals, and the FOFA (Future of Financial Advice) regulatory changes, have provided more insight into the Government's expectations and governance of Advice Professionals.

PIAA has created a potential educational barrier to the Property Investment Advice area, with the requirement to hold Professional Indemnity Insurance as the endorsement of professional practices.'
— PIAA

For you to understand the current state of the property market in Australia, in every state and territory, you need to not only understand what a property spruiker is, as outlined earlier, but also what a spruiker does.

Two-tier marketing is an example of spruikers at their best. This reportedly occurred widely in Queensland. People from 'out of state' were drawn into paying more than the locals, and the difference in price was shared among the employees of the spruiker, and other unscrupulous individuals assisting with the transaction.

A more recent phenomenon is that organisations are presenting seminars promoting themselves as being 'ethical' and 'educators'. Often these educators have properties they promote to their over trusting audience. It is often a front for undisclosed property interests, and the use of certain sales tactics to convert leads to sales.

Most property spruikers and property marketing companies use a property investment analysis tool. Whilst using a modelling tool is perfectly acceptable (and there is one tool most use, that I feel has value), it can, however, just as easily be used as a weapon. This tool can be used for bad just as much as it can be used for good. The unscrupulous users of this tool will intentionally mismanage expectations, mislead unsuspecting investors, and misrepresent data, thus manipulating it to get a sale. Many fields on this tool can be adjusted, but here are some examples of adjustments that are potentially quite inaccurate and misleading:

1. Entering a rental figure that may be inflated to make it look more appealing.
2. Lowering maintenance costs, insurance, rates, etc.
3. Only entering 80% of the loan-to-value ratio rather than 100%, if the investor is using another property as security, thus borrowing 100% of the debt.
4. Entering a very low vacancy rate, rather than being more conservative and cautious.
5. Stating that property has doubled in value every ten years, then using this as a predictor for the future, and entering a non-conservative capital growth figure.

The problem with the property industry, at the moment, is that there is no barrier of entry adequate enough, such as suitability to practice, qualifications of an educational nature, or minimum training. Any unethical business can sell property. There really needs to be an educational barrier of entry, and a regulator to regulate property practices. This would (I hope) eliminate unscrupulous property spruikers. It would professionalise the industry and standards, and offer better protection for consumers. Australian Securities and Exchange Commission ASIC currently do not have the authority to regulate real property. As I have already mentioned, property is not currently considered a financial product for the purposes of regulation. (Whilst property is of course a financial product, it is not considered a product under the umbrella of the financial planning industry and existing regulation in this industry). Thus, property is an unregulated industry at the point of writing this book.

I believe the Government really needs to draft legislation and implement it, to include property as a financial product, which then would allow ASIC to regulate the industry. The problem is that there are different industry bodies that are acting in their normal bureaucratic ways, and that have their own agendas, which differ to each other.

Legislation supporting consumer protection has some considerable limitations as to how it could apply to the property industry, and in particular property advice. There is no stipulation for advice that is appropriate to a person's circumstances. It does not stipulate that risks be clearly explained, or that a conflict of interest, if there is one — which often there is — must be disclosed.

Furthermore, it does not state that commissions must be disclosed. One firm, in 2013, made a public statement that 'it is their business how much they make, and no one else's'. In my opinion, this is completely unethical and exemplifies the mentality of many of these marketing companies whom take advantage of the general public.

Some of these spruikers and property marketing companies hire truly unethical salespeople. It is unbelievable what they get away with. Seeing such unregulated and unscrupulous behaviour was a catalyst to the writing of this book. It gives me enormous satisfaction to help others avoid these spruikers and others, who can scurrilously deal with investors without having any minimum knowledge or qualification requirements. An investment in property, you'll agree, is a big commitment, and some of these hoodlums have no respect for that!

Around 30% of Australians live in rental property. The Government, in many people's views, needs landlords to assist with housing the increasing population of Australia. The Government cannot afford to purchase thousands of investment properties themselves. Let's face it, they find it difficult enough to run the country. They, typically, take a short-term view on things, never making many real differences that last for generations to come. What matters to Governments more, on a global scale, is staying in office.

The Australian Government at any given time has one hand promoting one thing, and another that contradicts the first hand. One of the biggest contradictory examples is the fact they promote the importance of people working hard, to be more self-sustaining in retirement, yet they take away by limiting the pre-tax contributions into superannuation, thus effectively (and intentionally) inhibiting people from growing their superannuation. This is a double-edged sword. Firstly it allows the Government more money to service all those retiring on the pension, but it also works in reverse, to inhibit people from more effectively building their superannuation.

On a positive note people can, however, have more money available to invest in property, and take advantage of the better leverage available in property.

Getting back to advice

I have experienced and witnessed several examples of poor practice in the property market place. Unfortunately these are becoming more rife, and further entrenched, in the property industry. These poor practices lead to disenchantment and loss of confidence for property investors, who tend to become uncomfortable and can then resist continuing to invest as a result.

For example:
a) There is no regulation requiring that an individual, or company, disclose the commissions they are deriving from selling someone a property, nor is there a requirement for transparency as to any conflicts of interest or vested interests the parties have, in the property/ transaction.
b) There is no independent recognition of experience, or qualifications, of a property advisor to ensure the advice they are providing is coming from a sound base, and is prudent. Many so-called advisors are uneducated sales people, lacking in both life experience and industry experience.
c) Financial literacy is not taught in schools, leading most people to being open to exploitation.

Even when an industry does become regulated, such as mortgage broking, there are ways some brokers create perceptions, or manipulate the situation, misleading people to believe they know what they are doing, and that they are knowledgeable experts. Some are ex-taxi drivers, pet shop owners, or hairdressers who have had no previous banking experience. Thankfully, the mortgage industry is weeding these people out and, on the whole, most brokers do try to do the right thing.

There are several challenges and hurdles in regulating investment property. The simplest to overcome is dealing with the lack of integrity and character many of these sales people and companies possess. The more difficult issue is that many of these reports produced by the sales people involved, particularly for 'off the plan' (where often the projections lack conservatism), are open to interpretation. Reports are not often well researched, independent, unbiased or well referenced.

Often reports consist of all the lovely pretty parks and playgrounds in the area, and a few descriptions of proposed infrastructure and population increases. Rarely do they mention the supply of new stock in the area and its impact on the demand. The reports use emotive elements, and warm and cosy pictures. What they lack is real substance and true comparison made to other properties around the estate.

Another major problem is the fact that anyone can become a quasi-developer. Some information conveyed to potential buyers can be non-compliant and misleading. These developers can lack the infrastructure to adhere to all parts of the law, and they may also lack a team. The sheer diversity of property development would be difficult to regulate.

Over the years, the Government has undertaken several investigations, one of the most significant being a joint parliamentary committee investigation into property investment advice. The activities of 'less than ethical' operators out there, and spruikers, played a big part in why these investigations were undertaken.

Why engage the services of a true advisor?

Besides being independent of developers, marketing companies and property providers, we actively help people to avoid spruikers, *and* we research out-performing locations. To provide the best opportunity for investors to benefit from engaging our services, we tailor advice within the scope of a risk profile, which matches the client by comprehensively evaluating investment structures, investment property, property investment strategy, market conditions, and climate.

Considerable due diligence to the client, combined with property choices that have been researched and sourced, is provided in the form of a *Statement of Property Investment Advice*. We facilitate the ability for investors, who have engaged our services, to make informed decisions based on the quality of a foundation of information.

We take into account the investor's goals, their life style, and their finances, to find suitable property choices for their circumstances. We state all major assumptions similar to a financial plan or prospectus. All of our recommendations ignore emotion, and the emotive selling that the spruikers and most property marketing companies practise. Choices of property modelled utilize information of the product's potential performance, allowing for several property choices to be considered, as they may all meet the client's risk profile.

The main point to recognise here is this all culminates to reducing the urgency to purchase a particular property, and is therefore a more professional process. No glossy brochures with pretty pictures of all the wonderful inclusions — like stone bench tops, plush carpets, and shiny tiles. Most investors just want to know the property will have good potential to grow in value, will attract a good tenant, and will be affordable.

The model we use eliminates service level agreements with developers, which are currently used by many marketing companies. We help you by making sure you avoid situations where you might be given inflated performance projections, and experience pressure sales techniques that are designed to manipulate investors.

All this makes for a regulation-ready advisor, and addresses the concerns expressed by the Government, such as barriers of entry, consumer protection, and the big one, **fitness of individuals practising in the industry.**

In Summary

The Problems you can avoid
Traits of unregulated property advice personnel, led by many property marketing companies and spruikers (Beware! They can be one and the same):

- vested interests between mortgage brokers, banks, and associates
- undisclosed commissions
- no independence or objectivity
- not insured to give advice
- represent the seller — not you, the buyer
- have a property already lined up to sell, with heavy-handed sales techniques to entice you to 'sign up now'.

The Solution available

- you, the buyer, being independently represented, with no direct relationship with the vendor
- not having a property lined-up to sell. Property choices are guided by you, your goals, risk appetite, and finance
- all fees disclosed and work to a strict code of ethics
- no vested interests with the seller or their associates

- thorough research: analysis, not hearsay
- advisors with professional indemnity (PI) insurance (financial planners generally do not have this for specific property advice; property marketing companies normally do not either, when providing advice, they may only have PI insurance for selling you specific properties.)

The Value of this Solution

Modelling Tools are provided to help you

- reduce risk
- keep and improve your lifestyle
- have access to property you may not have had before
- gain explanations and education regarding risks
- leverage off the advisors education and experience
- realise that having a real property advisor is great insurance
- integrate strategies toward the goal of achieving a passive income in, or before, retirement.

Chapter 3

Buying the Right Property

'The great aim of education is not knowledge but action.'
— Herbert Spencer

Investment Property Strategy as distinct from Owner-Occupied Strategy

When purchasing a house to live in and call home, people typically buy with emotion. Investors who make bad decisions (and are normally unsuccessful in property investment) use emotion to purchase investment property, rather than allow the facts and figures to paint a more accurate picture. Some investors also want to be able to see the property, and smell it, and drive past. Investors don't do this with shares. They don't fly over to see Google. They don't knock on the door of Wesfarmers. It's ironic really, as all they are getting with share investments is a piece of paper — not bricks and mortar.

I have property managers to manage the properties I have. They organise maintenance that needs to be done. What would I gain by just observing the grass grow if I was to drive past? Maybe I might catch a glimpse of the tenant. If you're curious enough to 'people-watch', go to the local shopping centre.

If you do buy a property that you plan to renovate, subdivide, and actively engage with, then it makes sense that you would travel to it; this type of property investment is a totally different strategy to a strategy where you don't have time to improve or change or develop a property. It involves you being an active investor at some point — usually at the beginning. Time-poor investors do not need to purchase in their own state, but many will continue to believe they know best, and they will continue to end up with only one or two properties, and live on the pension.

Many states are worth considering buying in at any given time, but it changes, and it should not matter where you live in relation to where you should buy.

As this book is about investing in property, it is worth covering some useful information on property in general, for your benefit.

Shares Versus Property

Shares can make you a lot of money very quickly, but as various global downturns have shown, you can also lose it even faster. Investing in property, on the other hand, is a less volatile method for creating long term, lasting assets and wealth. Equity in property is still accessible. You don't have to sell it to access it — unlike shares. It's more tangible, and provides far greater leverage.

If banks think property is safer than shares, I wonder why investors do not necessarily think the same way. Banks will typically lend up to 95% for property and up to 50% for shares (sometimes going to a 70% maximum.) The reality is that a large percentage of companies that were on the stock market fifteen years ago no longer exist.

If you borrow for shares and the market drops, you would normally be asked to put in more money to top up your equity in the shares and, therefore, bring the exposure back to within the loan-to-value ratio that the bank provided you with originally. The loan-to-value ratio refers to the debt ($ figure of the loan) against your property, and the comfort the bank has in how much they want to consider providing you as a loan. The higher the loan against the value of the property the higher the exposure and risk is to the lender. With property, if the value drops, you wouldn't receive a phone call asking you to do anything.

Lenders normally don't do checks on the values of the properties they take as security. (When was the last time the bank valued your house, other than when you wanted a loan?) It's a known fact that people who borrow higher debt against the value of the property, in an under-performing suburb, can have their loan end up being greater than the value of the property. However, unless you asked the lender to do a valuation for a loan increase, you may well remain under the radar as it were.

Buyer and Vendor Advocacy

For as long as real estate has been bought and sold, a broker (more commonly known as a real estate agent) has been involved. Property can still be bought and sold directly between the owner and buyer, although this rarely occurs.

The problem is that both the vendor and buyer want the best price for themselves. The vendor wants the highest price, whereas the buyer wants to buy at the lowest price. The agent is necessary to advise on the 'market' value, based on sales of similar properties in the area, under normal circumstances. Selling and buying homes, for the purpose of living in them, is as much an emotional exercise as a monetary one. Vendors become very attached to their homes, through time and family history, and so may have an inflated idea of its value.

A buyer looks at the basics: bricks, mortar, location and price. For the buyer, family history is in the future. Thereby, a vendor can be, quite often, upset when offered a lower price than they believe their 'home' is worth.

Most buyers understand this and often feel uncomfortable in dealing direct with the vendor. The agent is the middle person whose job it is to negotiate a suitable outcome (i.e. the sale of the property.) The agent is paid a commission by the vendor, this being paid only when the property is sold, and the legalities are satisfied. Consequently, the agent is working for the vendor, not the buyer. The agent of course needs to find this buyer and convince them to buy. This situation can lead to a potential conflict of interest, as the buyer knows that the agent needs them in order to earn a commission on sale.

A common complaint from vendors is their perception that the agent, in convincing the buyer to put in a low offer to get a sale, is working more for the buyer, than for the vendor. The difference between an 'average' agent and a 'good' agent is the ability to negotiate the best price he can for his vendor.

In some cases, there may be more than one buyer for a particular property. This is the best case scenario for the vendor, and is the reason many properties are sold by public auction, whereby buyers can see the offers and bid accordingly.

The other main method of selling is by private sale, whereby all offers are submitted to the vendor. Under these conditions the offer is between the agent and the vendor and, under no circumstances, should this offer be communicated to a rival buyer. When more than one offer is on the table, the agent is obliged to advise the vendor of these offers, and be guided by the vendor's instructions. As you imagine, this system can be manipulated by an unscrupulous or lazy agent.

A third system of selling, a comparatively recent method, is by way of a sale by set date (also known as *set sale*.) This system offers the property by way of a suggested selling range, with all offers to be submitted by a specific date, at which time the vendor will consider all offers, and make a decision as to whether to accept the highest offer.

The other system is called a *tender process*, but this is usually limited to larger commercial properties. The main difference is that no 'for-sale' price range is displayed in the advertising.

In the past, agents advertised via printed media, such as daily and local newspapers, and with a 'for sale' board on the property. Potential buyers had to contact the agent in order to view the property. The advent of the internet radically changed the ways of marketing a property. Now the potential buyer can view all properties in their chosen area and price range, at their leisure, and at any time.

The information about the property is now very detailed, with colour internal and external digital photos, floor plan, land size, and even mortgage costs and median house prices in that particular suburb. As a result of this, agents now have to offer the property via 'open house'. The home is open for inspection at specific times, usually for half an hour on the weekend and once during the week. Private viewings are always available, but this is usually a follow up from an open house inspection. This form of marketing has become very sophisticated, with professional photography and copywriting the order of the day. This form of advertising allows many properties to be viewed on a weekend.

Also, in the past, agents tended to 'push' the auction method, as this gave them a larger marketing budget, and a guaranteed run of at least four weeks of advertising — and this led to the belief that auctions were more expensive. This is not the case today, and the marketing of a property should be very similar in order to attract a buyer. The only difference could be an auctioneer's fee, but again most agents don't charge for this.

When marketing a property, there are some fundamental facts that the agent should know. At any given time, there is a 'pool' of buyers looking to buy a home. This pool is large, but can be broken down into steps, such as low to medium prices, medium to higher prices, and high to expensive properties. E.g. In 2013, these categories would typically range from $300k to $500k, $500k to $700k, $700k to $900k, and then $900k to $1.2million, and so on. It is imperative that the agent gives the right advice as to where this property sits, and quotes a range accordingly. Otherwise, the vendor may be paying marketing costs of several thousand dollars for no result.

Some people selling their property (and I have seen it with families selling off deceased estates) choose the cheapest agent after obtaining a few quotes. This is unwise. The cheapest is not often the best. Why be 'tight' on the cost of marketing when it could lose you ten times that at auction, by going with a sub-standard firm? An extension to that could be the use of a sub-standard auctioneer, who could also result in a lower sale price.

When marketing, the agent should understand how buyers think and react. Most buyers (around 80% or more) check the internet and choose several properties to look at. Many buyers will then drive to the address and check out the neighbourhood. Good marketing should include a photo and text board, rather than just a plain 'for sale' board. This shows the buyer that the vendor is prepared to spend, and is genuine in their endeavour to sell. A plain board simply advertises that the property is for sale, and gives no indication of what this property comprises. The full photo and text board shows what the property has to offer and, more likely, the buyer will want to come back for an open inspection, or may be keen enough to ask for a viewing prior to the open inspection. A good board could cost between three and five-hundred dollars, out of a total budget of three to five thousand dollars, so it's money well spent. Some high-end properties could have a budget well in excess of this. However, the above figures are fairly average.

Some vendors feel that the agent should have buyers on their books and they don't need boards or open inspections (thus saving marketing costs.) Agents do have buyers on their books, and do sell homes in this way, but the reality is that over 90% of buyers respond to advertising.

Whether the property is going to be sold by auction, private sale, or sale by set date, most properties should sell in the first six weeks of listing — and do. The exceptions to this are in a 'down' market, where there are fewer buyers, and consequently more properties, or the price is too high. Some country properties can take longer to sell also.

The method of quoting a range is the best way of marketing. It is very difficult to put a precise figure on a property. Houses are like any other commodity, open to supply and demand, and some will attract few offers, whilst others may attract many. Large supply results in fewer buyers, and a lower price. Short supply equates to many buyers, and a higher price.

Demographics play a large role in this, such as migration, economy, interest rates, and first home buyers, etc. Quoting appropriately is crucial. Unfortunately, many agents tend to underquote a property to entice buyers. This method wastes the buyer's time and sometimes money (e.g. paying for a building/property inspection), and leads to the public being generally distrustful of agents.

There is legislation, in most states, that dictates how agents should quote — both to their vendor, and the public. In Victoria, an agent can quote a range to his vendor of no more than 10% difference, from the lowest to the highest (e.g. $500,000 to $550,000.) In quoting to the public, the agent can quote a larger range, but the bottom-end of the range cannot be lower than the lower figure he has quoted to his vendor (e.g. from $500,000 to any higher figure, such as $500,000 to $600,000.) In practice, most agents quote a range to the public of 15% (i.e. $500,000 to $575,000.)

Most agents quote, as their lower range, a figure of 10% below what they expect the property to sell for. (Most *buyers* end up spending around 10% more than they planned to when they first started looking.) This way, buyers have the opportunity to look at a property in their price range. Some agents consistently quote 20–30% below the true price range and property value, which is not only misleading, but illegal. Heavy penalties apply if they're caught. Some have been caught, but very few.

It is worth noting that, in some circumstances, a property in great demand can bring a much higher price than anticipated. This can happen when buyers are bidding at an auction and get 'carried away'. I am sure there have been many successful bidders with 'buyer's remorse' when things settled down and reality set in.

Anyone buying a property should set a budget and stick to it. If the property goes for more than this budget limit, walk away. There is always another property to suit. You must also understand the terms before bidding at auction. You cannot negotiate the amount of deposit, or settlement period, after winning the property.

Buyer's Agent

Since the 1960s we have been seeing a huge rate of population growth with the 'to be expected' growth in property, along with hundreds of estate agents offering a huge range of properties for sale, at any given time. Whilst there is more and more information available on the internet, many buyers lead busy lives, particularly in their work. As a consequence, many are time-poor and can't devote enough time to source their ideal property. This gives rise to a more specialised agent known as a buyer's agent. Some call them advocates. However, I believe there is a difference (to be explained later on). In this case, the buyer pays the commission to the agent to source a property. This can be helpful for buyers who live out of the area, interstate, or even overseas. Once the property has been found, the agent will negotiate with the vendor's agent, on behalf of the buyer.

A buyer's agent may be engaged just to bid at an auction either because the buyer cannot attend the auction, or to have a professional do the bidding to avoid getting 'carried away' (as some buyers have been known to do), and thus avoid paying too much for the property. At auction, many a buyer gets caught up in the moment, to find they have bought a property for far more than they are comfortable with, and later end up struggling with their finances. The difference here is that the buyer's agent is working for the buyer, as it is the buyer who pays the commission. In all other cases, the agent is working for the vendor (or should be).

Auction

Buying at auction can be a daunting process for many buyers, and understanding the process is essential. Auction rules stipulate that all required documentation be on display, the purchase be unconditional (i.e. no finance clause), and a deposit (usually 10% of the purchase price) be payable immediately by the successful bidder. There should be 'genuine' bidding only, with no 'vendor bids', unless specified by the auctioneer. The vendor usually has a reserve price, under which price they won't sell. The auctioneer will not disclose this reserve, but will usually indicate when it has been met, or exceeded, by stating that 'the property is on the market'. At this point, all potential buyers present know that the property will be sold to the highest bidder. If the property does not meet the reserve price, the property will be 'passed in' and negotiations will then take place, privately, with the highest bidder. The auctioneer will indicate to the buyer who holds the highest bid, and will call three times before announcing that the property is sold. The term used is that the property is sold on the 'fall of the hammer'. This is done to ensure that there are no late bids, and the buyer has the legal right to sign the contracts, usually straight after the auction.

Vendor's Advocate

Another recent specialist is an agent known as a vendor's advocate. In this case, the advocate is engaged by the vendor to look after his interests, in the selling process. As previously mentioned, there are hundreds of agents, with sometimes a dozen or more in any particular suburb. Selling a property today needs an experienced, knowledgeable, and ethical agent, to get the best result. Not all agents fit these criteria. Many agents overpromise and underperform. Others, who are fairly new to the real estate industry, may not have the necessary skills. Some agents just want a quick sale, which may result in underselling the property. It can be quite a minefield.

Many vendors invite three or more agents to submit their advice on price and marketing. This gives rise to a very competitive situation and, in order to get the business, many agents 'promise' to get a higher price than is achievable. The tendency is for the vendor to believe this agent and engage their services.

Most listings are exclusive for 90 days to that agent, and many a vendor has had to contend with weekly suggestions to lower the price, in order to sell. In many cases, once an offer is 'on the table', the agent will urge his vendor to accept the offer. In this case, the agent wants a quick sale, rather than further negotiating with the buyer in order to increase the offer. In most situations, as already mentioned, the marketing costs of a property sale can be two, or three (or more) thousand dollars, and this can be wasted by choosing the wrong agent.

The advocate, when engaged, is the 'head listing agent'. However, they do not market the property. They use their knowledge and expertise to engage an agent whom they judge to be the best for the job. An advocate may also recommend obtaining a 'sworn valuation' from a qualified valuer, to give an accurate assessment of the market price. Once this information is obtained, and the vendor wishes to proceed, the advocate invites the agent to work in conjunction with them, and it is then the agent's job to market the property accordingly.

It is the advocate's job to ensure the best method is used to market this property, and the advocate therefore monitors the process, and provides advice. The agreed commission is then shared between the advocate and the agent; a typical split would be 40% to the advocate, and 60% to the marketing agent. The advantage, to the vendor, is in having an advocate looking after their interests, and they do not pay any extra commission for this service. The advantage to the chosen agent is that he does not have to compete with many agents, and has the opportunity to be given multiple properties by the advocate. As with all successful sales, the agent will obtain extra business in his own right, as a result of the sale.

Selling a family home is a stressful business, and many vendors are wary of dealing with real estate agents. Real estate agents traditionally have a poor reputation and, in many cases, this is justified. Equally though, there are many experienced, hardworking and ethical agents who do a very good job for their grateful vendors. A good vendor's advocate can minimise this stress. It should be noted that an advocate should be a fully licensed agent, with **at least** ten years' experience as an agent. Anyone with less than these qualifications should not be a vendor's advocate.

Buyers Advocate

A buyer's advocate, in my opinion, is different to a buyer's agent. I will redefine the role of an advocate, for the purpose of my book, and how I see the industry changing.

A buyer's advocate sources property for investors on the back of in-depth research. They focus on helping investors rather than owner-occupiers, therefore reducing the wasting of time with emotion. They do not go to auctions for their clients. They do not negotiate, nor attend 'open houses'.

As an advocate, I implement the strategies I have designed for my clients, by researching outperforming suburbs, and locating the right type of dwelling in those suburbs. I then provide my client with choices of properties that suit the strategy. If a client does not want a strategy, the underlying function does not change. The important focus is reducing risk for the client. A true advocate, for the buyer, does not sell property.

Buyer's agents typically source what a client wants. They normally do not provide advice as part of their business model. Almost none of them are qualified to provide advice.

Chapter 4

Wise Choice/choose wisely ... TIP 2

'Nothing would be done at all if a man waited until he could do it
so well that no-one could find fault with it.'
— Cardinal Newman

Types of Contracts

Off the Plan

You sign an off the plan contract, today, for a property that may be twelve months to three years away from being completed. You would normally put down a 5% deposit, now, and the rest when it's completed. If you can't get finance when settlement is required, you will lose your deposit, and may face action and applied penalties from the property developer. On the flip side, this delay allows you time to save more money.

Many purchasers of these contracts apply for finance, to give them comfort that they can borrow the money. Of course, this comfort is somewhat superficial and actually, and ultimately, useless. Other than knowing what your credit history is by paying twenty dollars (approximately) to get your own report on yourself, it is a waste of the lender's time, and yours, to apply for a loan knowing the approval will expire **before** you settle. The approval will expire in 3–6 months from the time of approval. Your life could change over the time it takes to be ready to settle on the purchase. You will then need to re-apply for finance again.

Consequently, your original approval means absolutely nothing. All you really needed to do, originally, was go to a broker and gain an understanding of what your borrowing capacity is (at the time.) What it was and what it ends up being, two years later, when the property is complete and ready to settle, are two very different things.

In theory, the benefits used to be that you'd purchase something at today's price, and it will be worth more by the time it's built. The reality of late, particularly in areas with many developments going on (such as in Melbourne), is that there is a real risk the property developers have already factored a perceived increase into the price. Sales people (spruikers) and property marketing companies have been incredibly greedy, making upwards of 6% *and* bonuses by flogging these.

The other prevalent problem with off the plan contracts is that your chosen purchase is, often, a part of a complex building or development zone: one of many, largely the same in design, and/or newness. You then end up competing against all of the other people wishing to rent them out — and many attempting to do so at the same time as you. Some developers time the construction and completion of these developments in stages, and promote this as aiding to reduce the competition of trying to find a tenant, as they are coming to completion fruition at different times.

The reality is that your tenant may only sign on for six months, or a year, and when they move out you could well be competing with the next stage/release, and the dozens and dozens of other units now vacant and being advertised for rent. It risks becoming highly negatively geared due to you having to compete with those others looking to lease and, therefore, you having to reduce your asking rent price. There would, also, be no transparency as to how many investors, versus owner-occupiers, are buying in the building, so be careful. It could end up a slum!

Additionally, don't forget that at some time, in the future, you may want to sell the property, and by that time all of the apartments/ units **would have** been completed. You could then be competing against many others, in the same building, who are trying to sell their property. This competition will, then, lead to pressure on you to drop your desired asking price in order to compete with your fellow neighbours, and thus be forced to reduce your profit.

The benefits of 'off the plan' are the depreciation factors. The cost of the construction of your dwelling is often more than the value of the land. The value of the land, as a component of the price you paid, may only be as little as 10%. The building can be depreciated over forty years, and the fixtures and fittings over a seven to fifteen year period (on average.). There can be excellent savings on stamp duty, as you only pay stamp duty on the land value.

Yes, you can have some possible input into the inclusions, but who really cares? It's an investment, and you shouldn't over-capitalise (or involve emotion) in your choices of inclusions. You normally have more say in the inclusions for house and land packages. Some property developers promote the fact that you have more choice in the apartment, when buying into one of these 'off the plan' developments. This is a big disadvantage, thinly disguised as a benefit. Think about it: if you have a big choice, it obviously could mean there are many apartments, and less uniqueness with your particular dwelling therefore, there's potential for less capital growth.

With off the plan it's not all bad. On the contrary, many opportunities can be had. I, personally, made 50% on one unit over a three-year period, and many other investors have made good returns and great capital growth with off the plan developments. It really just depends where it is, how unique it is, and how much demand, in relation to supply, there is.

Many developers need pre-sales to make their funders happy, which presents an opportunity for savings by acquiring an off the plan dwelling at good prices.

Ensure you check what other developments are going to spring up in the area. Perhaps these others will cause over-supply, block your view, and so on. And do check the credibility of the property developer you're dealing with.

Compared to houses, units and apartments have a body corporate. The body corporate takes care of the common ground and maintenance. Tenants have less to do, and owners have less to concern themselves with.

Based on affordability, higher rental returns, the aging population, and less up-keep, units are becoming more popular. If you're an investor, though, be very careful **where** you buy a unit or apartment.

Let's face it and this goes for all properties, and I'm not endorsing one type of dwelling over others, most people don't invest successfully, or they're afraid of debt, **and** they may be limited by what they can borrow. Buying something is better than buying nothing, but only on the back of adequate research, of course.

House and Land

When purchasing a house and land package, the land content is normally approximately 30-50% of the overall purchase price.

Standard House and Land packages

It is most common to purchase a package, whereby you are purchasing the land from a property developer, and signing up to a construction contract with a builder. Mainly, these are sold as a package, and the builder and property developer are collaborating to sell them.

These contracts are less risky than off the plan contracts as, once the loan settles, you are no longer required to provide any further information to the bank for the purpose of the loan being approved. If your life circumstances change, you are more in control. You don't have the same risk as you would in paying a deposit and losing it eighteen months later if you can't obtain finance.

The downside is that there is a holding period where you have no income. You will have settled on the land and begun making repayments on the land. Normally, the construction contract always has five draw-downs, or progress payments, over the five stages in which the dwelling is built.

Example: Purchase price of house and land $380,000

Land price is $174,000
Deposit for land

The rest of the funds to complete come from the loan and your own cash/ equity, the amount depends on the LVR.	5%
Construction $206,000	
Deposit	5%
Stage 1 Slab	10%
Stage 2 Frame	15%
Stage 3 Lock up	35%
Stage 4 Fit out	20%
Stage 5 Certificate of Occupancy	15%

The above construction figure of $206,000 is broken down into pre-determined amounts, payable at the completion of each stage. The builder emails (or mails) the invoice, you check it, ensure it's correct, and then sign and forward it to your lender for them to pay. The process of building can take roughly 3-5 months, and each draw-down increases your debt, and therefore your repayments. You need to ensure you understand that you must be able to afford this holding cost. There will be no depreciation or rental income assisting you during this period.

There are, generally, never any body corporate fees with house and land properties.

There are some who will sell the concept of land appreciating and building depreciating. This is fine and correct, but, please don't be sold on this being the best and only way of investing. An apartment or townhouse, in a good area, will typically return more capital gain than a house in an average area.

Never forget the golden rule: anyone promoting any one type of property, or any one area, normally has a vested interest in the property, or a relationship with the property developer. I have questioned many property-marketing companies on this, and they simply provide a throw-away line along the lines of, 'Well, we have to make a profit too'. Some investment clubs or property groups charge a joining fee. This could be as much as $10,000, and then they can also make tens of thousands on the back end. There are many 'snouts in the trough'. Be aware!

House and land located in new estates, adjoining existing areas with known capital gain profiles, have the potential for steady growth. Families favour them, so researching the demographics is important. They are often lower in cost to maintain, with no body corporate fees, or costs for maintenance of common areas. However, you then rely on the tenant for the upkeep. Brand new houses attract a higher rate of depreciation based on how new the inclusions are, and repairs are minimized, compared to an older style property.

Be careful of what the contract states: some will not include everything required for a tenant to move in; others do, and these are known as 'turn key' contracts.

The turnkey items that get the property to a position of being ready to rent out include the following:

- Clothesline
- Letterbox
- Landscaping front, back and sides (Be warned that some contracts only include the front)
- Cooling and heating
- Flooring (Yes! Some packages exclude flooring and offer other inclusions instead, like landscaping)
- Curtains
- Security doors
- TV antenna
- Garage door motor
- Fences.

The real hassle can be the fences. You might have to chase down the name and contact details of the owners of adjacent properties — these could be vacant blocks of land and, naturally, you can't just knock on the door!

Some contracts require you to choose where all of your light and power switches will go. Others control where they go. This can take an entire day for some people, especially owner-occupiers who are normally completely emotionally engaged in their purchase.

These contracts have been the most popular for people in Australia over the years. From an investment point of view they, I believe, will lose their enormous appeal as the demand for smaller dwellings becomes more popular. The baby boomer generation, in my opinion, will wish to downsize to townhouses and units in built up areas, closer to transport and amenities, medical services, bowls clubs, hospitals, etc.. Therefore, the demand for these units and townhouses could well increase over the coming years.

The benefits of units and townhouses (I include duplexes and triplexes in this, as well as dual occupancies) will be affordability. People will continue wanting to live close to everything, and houses are not affordable for first homebuyers closer to the major cities. Actual houses are not as hassle-free as apartments and townhouses. Houses will generally bring-in less rent as they have more upkeep.

All capital cities have recorded lower yields for houses than apartments. Yet, according to the REIA, houses have generated slightly more capital growth than units over the last 10 years (by approximately 0.48% each year, on average.)

Land will continue to be carved up in the outer-suburban sprawl. Infrastructure will continue to be built but land itself is no longer the most important factor in a property investor's choice.

Highly placed authority figures in the real estate industry, in Australia, consider a house that is similarly priced to a unit, will be outperformed by a unit if it is good quality, and well-located. Investment units are returning a slightly higher return than houses bought at a median price.

Risks

Your property developer may not be able to proceed with the development within the time specified in the contract (e.g. bad weather may cause a delay). It is important you are able to continue to afford to make the repayments on the drawn-down debt, regardless.

You cannot inspect the property. Hence, you must rely on the professionalism, competency and honesty of the property developer, and the terms of the contract, to ensure the project is completed on time — and to an acceptable quality. The lender will, typically, only release the appropriate funds (on your behalf) when they are satisfied that works are completed and up to standard. This occurs at different stages of the erection of the building, by way of a valuation the lender arranges to be done.

You may be lucky and be able to purchase one completed as a spec home (not to be confused with a display home), a spec property is one that has been built by the builder on the speculation that it will appeal to many buyers. It does not have all the upgrades and luxuries that a display home would have and therefore is roughly the same value of the other properties being built in the area of equivalent size etc. They save you waiting several months for the construction of the property to be completed. The downside for the builder is they may not have a pre-sale on this property and therefore it ties up money they could have spent elsewhere. These are very difficult to source as they are very rare.

Display Homes

These are often in large new estates, but occasionally can be located in the middle of an established suburb. Display homes include all of the upgrades possible, to demonstrate how luxurious a property from that builder can feel and look. They showcase the supposed quality of the builder's product. These homes are always more expensive than the standard houses around them. They're the hamburger with the lot! Occasionally, builders sell these to investors, in return for guaranteeing rent for a year or two. The one benefit from this property type is the higher rent for the 'guaranteed rent period', as well as the upgrades and quality they contain.

There are several risks associated with these properties though, and most lenders don't approve of them. The valuation may not stack up. So, although the house itself (with all of the inclusions) is worth 'a figure', valuers' typically base a valuation on what a similar type property will sell for in the same area, based on comparable sales of similar properties, and usually within the previous three-to-six months. The display homes, therefore, may leave you short when it comes to settling on them. This will require you to put forward additional funds that, in turn, may have repercussions on your equity and cash reserves, affecting your next investment property purchase.

You could be over-capitalising (for the area the display home is in, as the guaranteed rent, or component of rent they are paying you, over and above market rent for the area, is built into the purchase price as well.) and it may take many years to eventually break-even, or for the market in which it is located to catch up, on top of that, builder guarantees are almost always a rip-off,

Whatever you do, you must not base your decision on any amount of guaranteed rent, as this amount of rent, although often higher than market rent, will only last for a limited time, and you must be able to continue to afford the property after this initial period.

Lenders that do lend on these (only a couple of lenders) will almost always ignore the guaranteed rent and use the market rent for determining if you can afford the loan.

Purchasing Established

Make sure you understand the contract, and whether there are any easements, covenants, overlays, caveats, heritage-listings, and/or other encumbrances on the property title. It could impact on what you can do to and with the property.

For Example:

I once looked at a property that had a block that was large enough to build another dwelling on the back. I checked the following with the local council:

1. Encumbrances — I discovered it was heritage-listed and I would not be able to alter the exterior. If I wanted to build another house on the land and then subdivide I would also have to conform to requirements for the style of the exterior of the existing house. The property could not be what I wanted it to be. The purchase would mean I'd have to match a certain style, and thus it would be more expensive.
2. The council laws regarding the minimum size of a block for the area and the zoning — This was okay as the block was big enough, and of minimum width for a cross-over (drive way). In this instance, the driveway size would be deducted from the size of each block. The point being, you must understand council laws.
3. Costs of renovating — It was a one-hundred-year-old house. The electrical wiring had never been replaced. What an expense this would have been!
4. Value of the land — If I carved the land up and sold it, taking into account the cost to build, seek approval, and all that is required, it would have been important to undertake a feasibility study of costs, and potential profits.
5. Check the zoning for building, sub-dividing capability, and cost and lending possibility — Some lenders will not lend money based on certain zonings.

The suburb was brilliant, the land size and the location of the block was perfect, the block was flat, and the property was not near power lines — but with all of the other feasibility analysis I undertook, it ended up not making commercial sense.

Generally, there should be amenities, schools, hospitals and transport in areas where you would consider purchasing existing property for investment. Being near a train station almost always trumps an area with no train station.

A risk profile may be low to moderate, but your risk is increased simply by not carrying out adequate due diligence and research. This does, however, apply to everything. Be aware that existing property has an additional, and different, layer of risk than new. Maintenance issues, repairs, and improvements all increase costs.

We have now looked at types of contracts such as house and land, and off the plan. These two types are the most common 'new' investment property contracts.

'90:10 contracts' are offered on house and land to conform to self-managed super fund (SMSF) regulation. You pay a deposit of 10% upfront, then 90% on completion; no draw-downs, as construction is not currently allowed in an SMSF. Off the plan is also an acceptable type of property to go into an SMSF.

Not every type of dwelling is suited to every type of investor. This, again, is why it is crucial that each investor seeks not just the right advice, but also from the correctly (and ethically) placed individual: one who represents the buyer; not the seller. Your chosen advisor should have a trusted relationship with you, and not the seller.

The type of dwelling, for you, the property investor, depends on your personal financial situation, your risk appetite, profile, and, in turn, your own goals and strategy. Everyone must have a strategy. The strategy can vary depending on your age and lifestyle; based on the stage of life you are at. The type of dwelling is determined, also, by the area in which you invest in, and your budget. It must also suit the demographic of the area.

There are always several areas to consider investing in. In some areas it is more worthwhile to purchase a unit, in others a townhouse or duplex, and in others a house. You need the dwelling that, after due research, suggests it may produce the best potential both now and in the future. The choice of area, though, is ultimately chosen based on research and the following three main criteria:

- Risk appetite and profile
- Financial situation
- Strategy

Whilst houses have more land, and units have less land, there is the on-going debate as to which is better. The answer: it depends. Whilst the land value is less than the component of land with a house (usually it is 10% for units, 20% for townhouses, and possibly 20-30% for duplexes), the move to urban areas is pushing prices up on units, and trending towards being closer to the price of houses. The unit owners are all benefiting from the percentage of land they own with the unit. Whilst they may not directly own a tangible amount of land, when buying an apartment they are still benefiting from the fact that the land, under them, will still be appreciating.

Other varieties of properties

Serviced Apartments

Banks will generally not lend you over 60–70% debt against the value of the serviced apartment you may wish to purchase. Capital growth potential is limited and is connected to the rental increase of the property. Some serviced apartment contracts have built-in rental increases over a given period of time. The rental increase directly affects the capital growth. The increase is, effectively, the capital gain. Do be aware that the value may not increase at the same rate, in the same time, as a normal apartment. Again, buy in the right area. Don't buy a serviced apartment just because it is a serviced apartment.

Serviced apartments can be good cash flow vehicles, but you must always undertake your normal research and due diligence as to where they are, how many there are in the location, and their proximity to amenities. You should also assess the floor area, and management fees. The fees can kill the deal.

The added risks with serviced apartments, over and above normal apartments, are the quality of the management service provider, the use of the dwelling, whether it can be owner-occupied, and the exit strategy. If it is difficult for you to get a loan, imagine the trouble you could have selling it down the line. Few investors want to plough in 30–40% of their own money, and many won't have that much money anyway. So don't think about it in terms of whether you can afford to do it; think of it in terms of how many others can just as easily do it. This knowledge could easily put you off.

The more money you have to put into this, the less money you have available to you to grow your property portfolio.

Some of the serviced apartment contracts require you to refurbish the dwelling, and this can be expected to be paid for every five years. It means you will have to invest approximately $5000 or more each time, and this may need to be spent just before selling the property, depending on how far into the next period you are. These refurbishments are required under the terms and conditions of ownership. The properties must maintain appeal for tenants.

Sometimes the management contract reverts to the owner, after five to ten years, which can eliminate the enforced requirement to refurbish. But, on the other hand, you then have to spend time and effort finding someone to manage the property on your behalf.

Student Accommodation

Student accommodation can be a good income earner, but is often very small inside (usually under fifty square metres). These property investments involve greater risk and may not be the appropriate choice. They don't have favourable capital growth, and lenders really dislike them (so they are difficult to get a loan for, and are also very difficult to on-sell to someone else, as it can be very difficult for the next purchaser to obtain finance as well).

Furthermore, as properties, they are not unique. The loan amount in relation to the purchase price is limited, similarly to serviced apartments. They are often the same as all of the others in the building. Often, there is a large supply of these and strong competition to rent and sell them. This could result in requiring you to lower your asking rent, and potentially lower your asking price when selling it.

If you don't want to build wealth and you only want cash flow then you may consider these. I, personally, would not.

Others

Other dwellings (which I won't spend much time on, simply because these choices may not be considered suitable for many) are resort style accommodation, studios, converted warehouses, kit homes and portable homes.

Kit homes can be a handy income earner, if you're adding it to an existing property with another dwelling there already. You can, therefore, gain two rental incomes from the one property (parcel of land). They are, however, very difficult to get a loan for.

Resort style accommodation can be good cash flow but very few lenders like them, and the re-sale market is limited. Their unreliable and inconsistent rental stream is also geared, mainly, from the high season.

Vacant Land

From vacant land, there is no income — except maybe agistment (agistment refers to someone paying you to keep their horses on your land) — and, therefore, no tax benefits from holding land. In many ways, vacant land ownership, as an investment property, is dead money that produces no immediate benefit, or help in affording the debt on it. Land appreciates and buildings depreciate, of course. That is what most spruikers will tell you as a throwaway line. Whilst I support the fact that land appreciates, it is used far too often in isolation with other realities, and is used by many who are liberal with the truth, and may generally lack independence and objectivity.

It is probably worth mentioning that buyer's agents, marketing companies, etc., have simply decided that their preference business model is to focus on one type of property rather than another, maybe as their knowledge is limited or they don't have the capability to diversify their business model. It may not only be a lack of independence. However, it leads to the same outcome. **You must deal with someone who does not limit themselves for whatever reason to just one type of property or location.**

Land can possibly be sold easier without a dwelling, as everyone has a personal preference for the type of dwelling they favour. It is also dependent on a person's budget as to whether they can hold the land, without income, before they end up building on it.

You must consider a lender's willingness to lend you the money as well. Typically, lenders don't like farm land and hobby farms or land over five acres. Always remember that if it's hard for you to obtain a loan, it will always be difficult for someone else to obtain a loan when on-selling, meaning it will be more difficult for you to sell. This leads to you reducing the price and losing profit. Do think carefully before purchasing acreage, or income producing land.

Focusing on vacant land, if a property is less than five acres in size it makes it easier to get a loan. You may end up paying commercial rates for any vacant land over five acres in size. The land serves no benefit in assisting your servicing, or in reducing your tax position, and so it negatively impacts on your borrowing capacity, and your ability to grow your property portfolio.

Can you afford to negatively influence your ability to borrow for future property purchases?

Can you afford the interest on the loan, with no immediate assistance or benefit provided by the land?

Do you want to pay the sewerage, council rates and water rates, with no income from it? If these services are not connected you may think you are being smart, but then again, it will be even more difficult to get a loan and sell it in the future.

When comparing a piece of vacant land to a piece of land with a dwelling on it, both land components, of the overall value of the property, will grow at the same rate (if they are exactly the same and all things are equal). So why not purchase land with a dwelling on it? Unless you can sit on your money for a long period of time, purchasing vacant land is not a useful strategy. You can always spend roughly $10,000 to knock the house down anyway, should you wish to.

Costs and Income	Land with a dwelling on it	Land only
Purchase Price	400k	180k
Borrow 104% (90% against itself, 10% and 4% costs against another property)	416k	188k
Interest on Loan (I/O) at assumed 5% pa	20.8k	9.4k
Holding Costs: (Rates, Insurance, Agent's commission, $300 maintenance) pa	4.5k	2.1k
Rental Income	20k	0
Tax Credit	9k	0
Total Holding Cost	-$870	11.5k
Rates are still payable on land. I have excluded insurance, and agent's commission, and retained $100 maintenance for mowing and upkeep. So if you had a dwelling in this example you would make $870 a year, but if it was land only you would lose 11.5k per year (ignoring tax implications on these figures)		

Industrial

These are commercial premises/buildings that have received a zoning suitable for industrial use. Often what they have in common is that they, generally, have an office space area, a working area (such as for heavy equipment, packaging, and technical pursuits like engineering), and storage. The suppliers of goods to the large retail stores would have an industrial space, or warehouse, somewhere. They can be found near busy and main roads — to allow better access to freeways, which makes transport easier — and on land that is farther out. These areas are deemed undesirable for residential dwellings, and are therefore cheaper.

If you have a steady and consistent tenancy they are good, with higher yields than residential property. Landlords of industrial premises may have more rights than those of residential property, but the contracts are different and require more depth of knowledge to negotiate.

Commercial

Commercial property may include a business, shop, retail, resort-style offices, factories, farms, and income-producing properties. The list goes on.

The values of the properties concerned are based on the rental returns. Often the tenant pays all the outgoings (i.e. insurance, rates, and fit out). This is a different market and requires different knowledge and due diligence. This type of property can be, possibly, good for diversifying your portfolio. It has typically higher yields.

Strata offices are becoming popular as people can rent them close to where they live, and it allows them to escape the distractions and interruptions at home, and expand their business at the same time.

(Strata title refers to a situation where the individual/ entity owns part of the property such as the dwelling, i.e. townhouse, unit or office, but they share ownership of the rest of the property such as some or all of the land, driveways, gardens, foyers, corridors in apartment buildings etc. Normally more than two dwellings that share a drive or common land require a body corporate/ owner's corporation to be established to insure the land and manage the responsibility of the shared areas. Caravan parks, resorts, retirement villages are more obvious examples of this.)

The problem with commercial property is its inherent lack of long-term, stable growth — just like the stock market, which is directly linked to the corporate world.

Many experts say that there is a high percentage of business failure in the first two years. Dunn & Bradstreet research shows that more than 80% of business failures are related to cash flow (rather than sales pressures), so vacancy rates can be high which soon offset the higher yields of around 8%.

Lenders will only lend you 60-70% for a commercial investment property, so you need more equity or cash reserves.

Resorts

These are typically studios, apartments or units. There are often a number of amenities on site and it is often not permitted to live in them. They are not for long-term tenancy. The properties are rented out on an ad-hoc basis, as casual holiday rentals. Whilst you do not have an all year round tenant, you can earn great yield on the times that it is rented. This is during holiday periods, and holiday makers pay a huge premium to rent these out due to the amenities, location and time of year.

Similar to serviced apartments, the property management of resort investment properties can be the biggest risk. Management fees can be exorbitant, and your management can be unreliable and incompetent. You may be required to do a new fit-out every few years and, even if you are not required to do so, you may feel pressured to upgrade your property's image, in order to continue competing for tenants with other owners, who may have recently upgraded the fittings and fixtures in their rooms.

Fractional Ownership, Consortiums/Syndicates, and Time Share

I am not a fan of any of these. A number of investors have been pulled into buying in consortiums in the past, and often through unscrupulous sales companies. Syndicates are risky and involved. There are a number of other investors involved who own shares in a company (or companies) that, in turn, own the properties. What if the company ends up going into liquidation? It may be very difficult to reclaim your investment capital. Risks can be managed, to some degree, and these can help obtain high yields but, again, you are best to seek professional advice.

Time share properties can be helpful if you are the sort of person who wants to go on holiday to the same place every year. Some will allow you to stay in a different place every year, which I suppose can be useful. But do calculate whether these property investment types are worth what you pay for them. Investing in time-share depends on your personal situation and travel interests.

Fractional ownership allows you to purchase 'into' a property (such as a good quality holiday home at an expensive ski resort) that you may not be able to afford wholly by yourself. You pay an annual fee (similarly to a time-share), allowing you to stay there every year, for say four weeks, with the possibility of some additional weeks, on request.

You purchase shares in a unit trust that owns the property. Further down the line you can sell your unit share, or the trust may sell the property, dispersing any monies you are entitled to for your share.

Chapter 5
Choosing the right STRATEGIES ... TIP 3

'If you plan on being anything less than you are capable of being,
you will probably be unhappy all the days of your life.'
— Abraham Maslow

Active (the strategy is not just buy and hold; you need time and effort)

Non-passive or, rather, active investment is a quicker way to generate capital growth and cash flow. I am in favour of this strategy if you have time but it still requires considerable research.

This strategy is not necessarily appropriate for a time-poor individual who lacks knowledge on this topic. There have been several stories given to me, and while some are good, many are of failure and cost blow-outs, resulting in people losing interest in property investment, in general, just because of one mistake they have made.

Making Capital Growth Happen Now

This can be achieved in several ways. The three main ways to achieve capital growth include renovating (to improve the value of the property then selling the property), sub-dividing to create another title, or strata-titling (such as developing to include three or more units on the one title, and then applying to council to separate the dwellings onto their own titles, and then keeping or selling one or more of the properties involved.)

Sub-Dividing

Almost anyone can do this with the right-sized block of land, in the right area, by applying to council to split the block. Sub-dividing the one block may mean that you create two more smaller land lots with individual titles; you can then create smaller developments using the property. With large developments it could end up being *thousands* of smaller titles. Bear in mind that a property does not, necessarily, have to be sub-divided to build more than one dwelling on the land, you can strata the titles.

This is a good form of property investment if you have time. It can be very profitable, but also quite risky. There are a number of considerations, the main one being to undertake a feasibility analysis.

Below, I have included some costs to take into account when determining the financial effectiveness of this exercise.

Your profit is derived from the sale price less the following costs:

- Purchase price and stamp duty (to begin with) and, naturally, as per any property, all of the adjustments at settlement that a good conveyancing professional will handle for you (typically priced at around $1000.)
- Interest from the loan
- Design
- Engineering
- Surveyor
- Compliance
- Bank fees
- Project management fees
- Contingency fees
- Land holding costs

- Civil engineer
- Architect (the architect can manage the town planner, surveyor, Engineer, geotech and landscape)
- Builder (if you have a good builder they can manage the concreter, carpenter, plasterer, painter, bricklayer, electrician, and plumber.)

Further, you need to consider water, sewerage, power, storm water, and so on.

Check the distance that the building has to be from the boundary, precedents that have happened in the area (similar to what you want to do), and zoning — to determine the chances of approval from council.

Establish a minimum lot size, driveway width, steepness of block, and environmental impact.

Assess timing considerations with the site — due diligence, feasibility, finance, acquisition (if you don't already own the site), development approval, building, and whether or not to eventually sell or keep the site/s and rent it/them.

Just as with house and land packages, I recommend you always avoid non fixed-price contracts. You must have a fixed-price contract. Some contracts can be based on hourly or cost-plus rates. Never expose yourself to such risk! My brother-in-law is a builder and he warns his clients about these risks. Many builders are not as ethical and may just take advantage of you.

Stata Title

'Strata' was defined earlier under strata offices and the definition applies here. This strategy is a favourite as it takes less time than a subdivision and construction, and there is less involved than construction.

The shorter you hold it the less expensive it is. Strata titles are great for generating immediate value, as you can then sell the separate parts off. You have probably heard the saying 'the sum of the parts are worth more than the whole'. An example is purchasing, let's say, four lots on one title, and then applying to separate each title, thus allowing you to sell one, two, or all of the lots, and/or keep some.

Consideration may include taking into account separate services, such as electricity, water and gas supply, what the fire rating is of each dwelling and the walls in between, allowance for parking, wiring, step height, insulation, and balcony rail height. Many of these things may fail current council regulations and may have to be implemented to adhere to current regulations.

Renovation

Many renovators do not make money, as they can either under-estimate the budget required to complete the job, the time required (and then rush the job), or they do not understand what will add value, nor what it is that is important to retain (based on where the property is.) An understanding of the local market is very important, which is why many successful renovators focus on two or three areas/ suburbs that they understand. The renovation project also needs good management. There are excellent educators running training programs, who charge $5,000 to $10,000 to teach you what you need and want to know. You also need to weigh up the time you have to implement what you learn. Just as life gets in the way of most people growing a property portfolio, it also gets in the way for most people to implement what they learn — which then leads to the realisation you have just wasted $10,000. Many people spend this money on training, then go back home full of excitement, to find that routine sets in.

Renovation knowledge is very important, but, if you don't practise or start, you may soon forget what you learnt. Of course, cosmetic renovations can be much easier than structural, and require less time and money. Educators make their 'cookie cutter' approach sound so easy. The difficult thing, besides finding the time to carry out your new found interest, is mainly in locating a suitable property. This is something almost no educator will help you do. If they do, you must question whether they have vested interests.

It is easy to locate something 'under' market value, but is it in a close enough location to you, so you can carry out the renovations? Is it cost effective? Is there enough profit margin in the project? These things can be calculated, but you need the right property first.

In Australia, it no longer surprises me to see, time and time again, people renovating their home, only to then put it on the market. Some people live in environments that may be considered unfit for most of us. They spruce up the property to increase the potential sale price, but it is really sad that some of these people just don't renovate to enjoy their house more. Why only do it when you want to sell? Why not enjoy the benefits of your labour and money spent?

Here lies a basic formula:

Purchase price

Plus

Purchase costs

Renovation costs

Holding costs

Selling costs

TOTAL costs =

Sales price

Less Capital Gains tax

= Net Profit.

You need to determine if you are happy with the proposed end result, and in the proposed time it would take. Bear in mind there will be tax consequences in selling the property in less than twelve months. There will be no capital gains exemptions. Likewise, it could be construed that you are in the business of property development, and also lose your capital gains exemption, amongst other things.

New Versus Old

New property does have its benefits and downsides. I have used this strategy of buying new as it suited me, but am now moving into existing, I like both. I achieved higher rents and it was more appealing to tenants. New property basically has greater market appeal. Most people, in my opinion, would want to rent new if they could. Why would they want to rent old if they could avoid it?

New contains the latest, or newer, technology. The downside is they are more expensive to purchase, you are paying above median house price/median unit price in the area, and you are getting something smaller for your money.

The size, though, is relative to a given area. Often a unit can be better in a particular area than a house, and vice versa. Of course, it may be of benefit to you to purchase a two-bedroom unit in some areas, which you may be able to afford to do, if it is older (compared to a new one-bedroom unit for, possibly, the same price.) This, however, may be mitigated by new property having greater market appeal.

Newer properties may have issues. They may have been more poorly constructed, as compared to how builders made older houses, but they may also come with a seven-year builder's guarantee.

Existing property allows you to negotiate and, more importantly — if you are not just a time-poor investor and you have time to spend on your property — it can be great for increasing the value of the property, rapidly, by improving it.

Existing properties can be cheaper, but can have far less tax benefits, with dwellings constructed pre-1987 ineligible for depreciation. Fittings and fixtures may be old as well and, therefore, give you less depreciation opportunity which, in turn, does not reduce your tax as much — which means you have higher holding costs. This higher holding cost may be compounded by receiving less rent, due to its lower appeal to as many potential renters. There is a greater risk of required repairs and maintenance as well.

You can buy older property anywhere of course, whereas, there may be some areas where there is limited new property for sale. If there is an abundance of new property, and it exceeds demand, then reconsider your choices.

Negative Gearing

*Basically this means you b*orrow money to buy an investment property where the interest cost and other expenses to maintain it are not covered by the income. The difference/ shortfall may be deducted from your taxable income.

Sustaining a loss now, in turn, can offset income and produce a tax deduction, which aids you in holding the property over time. Older property will have less depreciation/tax benefits and will be more negatively geared. As you leverage, you have more debt using other people's money. More debt costs more, which may end up in the property being negatively geared. Sometimes it may cost nothing, or it may cost several hundred dollars a week, depending on how well you've done your research, and what it is you are trying to achieve. In the case of the property costing several hundred dollars a week, it may be more a matter of what are you looking **not** to achieve.

If you want a future, you need to invest for the future. This will involve investing money. The cost of holding an investment property can be minimised with the right property, but, if it does cost you to hold it, it can be considered a forced savings plan. If you invest $2000 a year, or $5000 a year, it is better to spend this toward property as it allows you to control an asset worth several hundred thousand, versus shares, where you only make money on the money you invest — not on the $400k property price, for example. I am not for or against negative gearing, as it serves a purpose and cannot be avoided for an investor who is seeking to build wealth rather than only cash flow (and not wanting to be active in improving or changing the property.)

Positive Gearing

This is straightforward: the income is more than the outgoings.

Property Risks

Growth Investments

Property is a long-term investment. You should avoid holding it for short term, although the property type can determine the length of time. The longer you hold the property, the less the impact of short-term fluctuations.

Reduced Liquidity

Unlike shares, property cannot be sold as quickly, meaning your money is tied up for a period of time that could be significantly longer than for shares. However, having a redraw –monies you have paid over and above your repayment commitments for that loan, and which may be sitting in the loan or facility linked to the loan allowing you to access these monies — facility can overcome this.

Risk of not Diversifying

Spread your risk — the more money you invest in one investment the more it is exposed. Property choice impacts on long-term returns for your property, property portfolio, and capital.

Tenant Risk

There may be times your property is untenanted, such as between leases, and it could take time for a replacement tenant to be found.

Interest Rate Risk

The cost of interest is an inherent feature when leveraging/borrowing money to invest. The cost versus benefit dynamic can change when interest rates increase. Buy smart, to begin with, in order to better manage risk.

Investment Risk

The value of your asset could fall and, depending when you sell it, you could get back less than what you invested.

Market Risk

There is volatility in the property market, albeit less than the share market. Prices can go up and down. You need time to balance out this risk. Don't sell if the market is down to avoid a capital loss.

Overall Purchase Risk

Avoid being emotionally involved when calculating a property investment risk, over using business sense and a commercial view point. It's like running a business. You should **not** listen to your friend, neighbour, or the media, about how to run your business. You run it based on the numbers. Property should not involve innuendo, hearsay, guess work and, most importantly, it should not involve what you pick up at a friend's house over a few drinks and a barbeque. If you base a decision on an opinion you almost certainly guarantee failure. It involves research, due diligence, facts and figures, trends, and other data. Every business has processes, procedures, a business plan and strategy, desired outcomes, targets, and (maybe) employees. Businesses have tangible goals and targets; not intangible ones.

You need a plan/strategy in order to achieve a task, process, job, or goal. Plans and strategies are not stagnant. They can change. They're tweaked, optimised, flexible, and accommodating. There are many different strategies in property investing. Some are better than others, and some are just different. Some are more suited to time-poor investors, whilst others suit hands-on type investors. I don't think you should use just one strategy. You need a balance.

With a business you need to get the numbers right. You need to do research and due diligence to reduce risk, and reduce exposure to poor decisions. You cannot afford to be complacent. Many investors, however, don't understand the data they have in front of them. They misread the facts and they fail to take into account all of the costs when determining their cash flow or holding costs. This is why you need advice.

Costs

There are two main groups of costs:

Buying costs

Buying costs include:

- Conveyancing
- Stamp duty
- Loan Mortgage Insurance (LMI) (possibly)
- Land tax (possibly)
- Adjustments with rates
- Delays with settlement (possibly).

Holding costs

Holding costs include:

- Rates
- Insurance
- Body corporate (possibly)
- Maintenance
- Repairs
- Agent management fees

WARNING

There are some multi-layered property spruiking firms around that will arrange the loan, the conveyance, and the contract for you. Obviously, my main concern is the fees they charge: not only on the interest rate (to provide themselves with a very healthy profit margin), but also with conveyancing costs (quoted to me, from a couple of these firms, at around $2000.) Then you have the sign-up costs (which can be around the $8000 to $10,000 mark), and then the back-end commissions (of $25,000 to $50,000 or higher, depending on whether it is their own land they are selling you.) They sell you this idea by saying how easy the process is if you use them. They offer to do everything for you, but it is more costly, often unethical (from many points of view), utterly unnecessary, and something I would avoid at all costs. They may also have a relationship with some valuers they use to support their potentially inflated prices.

I quote Terry Ryder below, which sums up everything wrong with the industry. Terry and I were spending some time together at one of the Melbourne Home Shows, and it became apparent that many investors believe that, in order to buy new property, they have to buy property from property marketing companies. We noticed all manner of beasts at the Home Show. There were American property spruikers, high capital growth prediction spruikers, developers with their own little slick salesmen, other stands who hired models in tight pants and short skirts, and one major player with advertising on television and offices throughout Victoria. The latter was one of the biggest con artists of them all.

'One prominent predator at last weekend's home show learnt all he knows from one of the industry's most notorious spruikers, who runs what I term the industry's most vertically-integrated rip-off — charging a huge fee for their advice, before recommending that clients buy product developed by the spruiker, get their finance from a related company, and then pay maintenance and management fees from another related business.'
— Terry Ryder, in reference to the 2013 Investor Home Show

Think before you leap!

Optimizing your property investment portfolio

Optimizing the performance of your property investment portfolio will be a key component for any investor looking to maximise the return on their investments. Optimization can be done using a range of strategies depending on the type of property(s) you have and the desired outcome you are trying to achieve. The common denominator will be either improved performance of the asset — be it capital growth, manufactured equity, or additional income — or improving the structure of your loans.

Your loans can always be reassessed at and, depending on the type of loan, you can rework your servicing to maximise your borrowing capacity and cash flow in relation to interest cost.

Historically, property has proven to be a great asset for capital growth over time, and the compounding growth effects of this can be quite phenomenal. Anything you can do as an investor to assist this process will reward you well, and, in most cases, the longer you hold the asset the greater the reward. However, short term, if you can minimise holding costs and maximise rental income, the better you can handle any changes in your lifestyle (from change of job, to more children, etc.)

Value adding to a property is a great way to fast track the performance of a property. This can be done in many ways; they include increasing the use of the property by sub-dividing the land, obtaining development approval for multiple dwellings, as well as making improvements to the existing dwelling to increase its value and appeal. Quite often, any of these options can quickly increase the value of your property, which will improve the compounding growth of your property as well as provide equity that can be potentially used for future investment opportunities.

As well as increasing the value of your property, optimization will also come from implementing strategies to increase the cash flow from your property(s). This can certainly be achieved by reviewing your loan structure as mentioned. It can also be done (as mentioned above) by developing the property and renovating it: more properties on the site means more rent, and a more appealing property will most certainly result in higher rent. There are also cash flow specific strategies that investors can utilise, like offering the property up on a rent-to-buy scheme or vendor finance contracts. This will be discussed in greater detail at a later stage. These types of strategies will generate a much larger weekly return on the property, but the trade off to this will be relinquishing the right to much of the capital growth in the property over time.

Case Study

'Not long after purchasing my first property it became clear to me that I had a real affinity with real estate and it was going to be an asset class I would focus on and use as an investment strategy. For me it just made sense because to get started you didn't need a huge amount of capital, and the investment produced income that assisted with the costs associated with holding onto the asset. For me, the plan was to purchase as much real estate as I could sensibly afford and put in place the strategies required that would enable me to hold the assets long term and get the benefit of the capital growth over time. It was these plans that lead me to understand and implement optimization into my investing.

'To execute my plan I needed both capital growth strategies as well as income strategies to make it work. Capital growth was required to create equity that I could use to purchase more property, and income was required so I could afford to hold onto the assets long term. Each property I would buy may not achieve both requirements (although in some cases it would) but the intention would be that either reasonable growth or reasonable income would result from the purchase.

'The types of properties I would purchase geared more towards growth were properties I felt had great value and opportunity. These would include properties that I could renovate, properties that I could complete a sub-division on: blocks of units that I would purchase on one title and be able to separate into multiple titles, as well as properties that I considered had great future capital growth potential. They might be properties that I considered were in growth corridors in capital cities, under-performing suburbs surrounded by performing suburbs, rural towns that I believed had bright futures, and mining towns.

'With regards to properties purchased geared more towards cash flow, interestingly, many of the properties I purchased for growth generated great income as well, particularly the blocks of units on one title, some of the rural towns, and most of the properties purchased in the mining towns. The most powerful cash flow properties for me though were properties I purchased and then sold on vendor terms contracts. This was a real game changer for me because up to the time when I first learnt about this strategy I was always struggling to meet my cash flow objectives. Vendor terms contracts are a true income strategy and it couldn't have come at a better time for me then just prior to the GFC when interest rates where rising rapidly which, in turn, increased the holding costs across my portfolio.

'The result of implementing these varying strategies was that I was able to achieve my objective of purchasing many properties that I was able to hold onto. The goal was to build a portfolio that would financially look after itself, and I am comfortable enough now to say that I have achieved that goal. Of course you have to constantly monitor the performance of each property and implement any changes accordingly to adjust for any changes in performance should they occur.'
— **Garry Harvey**

Optimization may well be different for each investor, but the importance of it will be common to us all. I think when you are clear about what you want to achieve, have a team in place, a strategy, and a plan, the goal you have will be much more tangible and achievable. Learning and understanding the various investment options is critical, but seeking advice is a must, because it enables you to have and implement the right strategy to achieve the outcome you are looking for.

Check out my interview with Garry Harvey, a serious investor

http://www.austpag.com.au/premium-content

RESEARCH ... TIP 4

Plan to Succeed

What is research and due diligence? Everyone seems to have an answer to this question.

Many investors are drawn towards innuendo, media hype, and listening to friends, family, and backyard experts. Everyone has an opinion. The real issue, which inadvertently leads to failure, lies in not undertaking proper research. Some people kid themselves into believing that just reading a glossy brochure about some 'house and land' package or 'off the plan' project is sufficient, and that the salesperson is possibly believable and trustworthy. I strongly beg to differ!

There is no real rulebook out there.

Here are some respectable and risk-reducing considerations that should make your job easier in finding an outperforming location, which reinforces why it is important to seek objective advice.

I believe advice is only objective if it serves the person being provided the advice. It should have nothing to do with any vested interests the advice provider has. It has nothing to do with the belief system, attitude, or religion, of the person who is providing the advice.

The advisor cannot be engaged by the vendor. Preferably, they should not directly communicate with the vendor. They should not have a contract contracting them to market-specific projects, or have targets or (key performance indicators) KPIs to achieve for anyone.

Objective advice should be based on facts and figures, and reliable information — *unbiased* information. This goes for information provided to the investor, and the information the investor is basing their *own* decision on, as well. Often property investors can fall into the trap of using their own emotion, beliefs, attitude, and experiences to base decisions on, such as where to buy and what to buy, and the inclusions in the property itself.

Every decision I make is based on what I have learned, discovered, or researched, and this will assist in calculating the potential of the location and property to make more money. What I *personally* prefer has no relevance compared to what the area suggests I need, in reference to the type of dwelling in the area that I should purchase.

What the demographic wants, and what I should be spending for the type of property in the given type of area, is what's important.

Components of Research

Let's start with the reality of the situation with any property. There is no guarantee.

There is no magic wand. Some sell answers to what they call 'secrets'. There are no secrets. However, if you don't do your research you are planning to fail. By researching you are, in effect, reducing your risk by eliminating some very obvious negatives that could be associated with an area. This serves to reduce your chances of failing, and therefore increase your chances of success.

'If anyone presents themselves as a holder of "secrets" in real estate, run away. Don't look back. Anyone promising to reveal secrets in the property business is, by definition, a spruiker.'
— T Ryder

Looking at supply and demand again, many marketing firms and spruikers (who have vested interests in specific locations, due to their vested interests in, and incentives attached to, specific projects) will tell you how good the population migration is to the area and, maybe, what the Government are planning to spend. They excite you with the fittings and fixtures included in the project, and this can lead to many investors immediately forgetting that every other apartment, in the building or house in the development, has the same or similar inclusions.

The major hole in their story is what the supply and demand is in the area. They tend to ignore this fundamental part of research, and conveniently misrepresent population migration. It is misrepresented, as it is not taken into context with supply and demand by almost all of these spruikers.

The location of the suburb is a good starting point. Its proximity, to some, is the driving force attracting people to the area. If people are not attracted to the area, why would the area increase in value? The fundamental figures start with supply and demand, like any commodity. If there is no demand, then it has little true value.

Some places have the benefits of a sea change; some have the benefits of the country.

The more important elements of the location are its infrastructure.

Some infrastructure is merely 'being discussed' by council, and other authorities, as to 'whether it will be planned'. Then it may end up 'being planned', and move forward to being a 'committed plan'. Once the infrastructure has actually commenced, you can be certain that it is in full swing and it will have a tangible end result. The best solution here is to select a location where there are several existing industries. Be careful if you're acting on something that is only being discussed. It needs to be approved.

Mining towns may only have mining as an industry, and can help you make excellent money, but you can also lose a great deal — not just in capital growth potential, but through real growth decline. Rental property often declines significantly in a 'one industry' town. If the industry falters, the town could die. You need a location where people will stay if an industry dies.

The economy of the area and surrounds, including the amenities there already (and in the pipeline), are important to know. Properties in

85

suburbs with train stations tend to grow more than suburbs without stations in metropolitan locations. Hospitals, schools, other transport, and shops are important too.

The demographics, particularly for guiding you in making a more informed decision about the 'what' you should buy in the area, are very important for your budget, growth, rental, and any works needed on the property, and whether those renovations will improve the value. It also tells you the number of renters in an area. It is very handy to know if you can find out how many investors are buying in the same development you are looking at, and over what time frame the dwellings are being released.

In some areas, units are more popular and will have appeal to a greater percentage of the population. In other areas, duplexes or houses are better.

Vacancy rates (and not just the current rates, but how they are trending) will help you see if the area is becoming more popular, or losing people. A simple snap shot will not demonstrate this, as it only captures a moment in time. When you look at shares you would normally look at trends, so why not do the same with property? The methodology applies to the following points:

- Capital growth history
- Yields
- Days on the market
- Discounting and auction clearance rates
- Median house prices
- Population
- Supply and demand

Research at State level

Narrow down to the location, based on borrowing capacity and strategy, **bearing in mind the basics of supply versus demand, in conjunction with population growth,** and infrastructure that is supporting employment and employment growth. It must be a multi-industry suburb to avoid excessive risk. Check, also, whether the infrastructure growth is temporary. Will people leave once everything is built (i.e. trades people, construction workers, etc.?) Will vacancy rates increase after the construction of infrastructure is completed, particularly when developers moved in like moths to a flame and over-develop an area?

Check the position that state is in, in regards to the property cycle — property cycle referring to the period of time over which the price of a property changes by being influenced from demographic, economic and supply and demand changes in the area; each area may have it's own cycle and be at different stages than any other area — and whether it is at the bottom, middle, or top of the cycle. It is always a good time to buy, but *not* everywhere, at any given time.

Oversupply, master-planned communities, and excess land can all hinder growth. Prime examples could be suburbs in growth corridors, as there could be better opportunities to be had further in towards the CBD, or even in locations the same distance from the CBD in some cases. In some of these large estates schools, hospitals, shopping centres, and a train station are all aiding the benefits of your potential property. Trains and access to transport are big factors in the investment being viable.

If you follow this process, you will dramatically enhance your ability to time the market better, take more advantage of out-performing potential, reduce the risk, and balance the effect on your lifestyle — and better your future! I have only covered some simple basics here again.

Chapter 6

Game Plan ... TIP 5

'There are risks and costs to a programme of action, but they are far less than the long range risks and costs of a comfortable inaction.'
— John F. Kennedy

Let's address some strategies, bearing in mind that they all have their merits but may not suit everyone. I have split them up under time-poor and active investors.

You can have one plan and one strategy for getting you from A to B, but you need to consider several sub-strategies — all working in unison, and complimenting each other — successfully accomplish the bigger picture.

Time-poor Investors

1. House and land packages

Many vertically integrated sales firms promote this strategy, on the basis that land appreciates and buildings depreciate. They use some basic facts and twist them, or rather focus on them while ignoring all others, typically for their own gain and to support their own vested interests: because they make more money. Sometimes they are the property developer. Sometimes they have 'under the table' deals going on, or they have simply decided that their business model will work one way or another. Possibly it is easier for them to train simple people in how to become good sales people, focusing on one product, because it may be too complicated for the (often) unscrupulous salesperson to intellectually cope with selling more than one type of product.

I would much rather purchase a well-placed unit or apartment than a poorly placed house. I could not care less how much land was involved, based on this approach. This is a great strategy, but buyers beware! When the firm is flogging this as the only strategy, they will almost always be trying to sell you a piece of stock they have on their books.

Yes, they have house and land packages there waiting for the unsuspecting buyer to purchase. One firm charges $10,000 to become a member and for them to offer you a property, and then a further $6000-$8000 per property, on top of your membership fee. I once happened to be in the same room as one of the directors of such a company, and he mentioned that I did not need to pay this joining fee as it was easy to do it on one's own. He said people simply lack confidence to do it themselves, and want to pay someone to do it for them. He also said they often make $25-60k per transaction (depending on if they own the land themselves, which they often do.)

I even received a call from one of their telesales people, who was quite aggressive when confronted with the lack of ethics involved in charging clients at both ends (i.e. charging the client a fee, and also receiving a commission on the other end.) He simply, dismissively and defensively, stated that we all need to make money. I was bowled over at this blatant disregard for integrity and ethics. Besides this fact, how can they legally (or ethically) truly represent the client if they sell property, represent the seller, or are in fact the seller?

Be aware that a property marketing company's property division will, typically, be under a different name than their sales division, development division, and mortgage division, etc. They would own one legal entity (which they own the land through) and then sell through another legal entity, therefore creating the illusion of two independent bodies. Of course the connection with all these entities is in small print somewhere, but how many people read this?

I support 'house and land' as a strategy, in conjunction with other strategies. The 'where' and 'when' is important though, as is the type of house.

2. Off the plan

Again, I have no problem with this type of property within a strategy. However, this statement must be qualified.

Marketing companies specialise in this type of investment. They use techniques, such as myopically focusing on population growth and proximity to the CBD, as impulse factors to influence a buyer's decision. They work on motivating someone to channel their own focus on the logic of what is being said, rather than the logic being qualified (or expanded upon) and put into reasonable context and accuracy. Other forces present in the market are intentionally ignored. An example of this is Melbourne's Docklands — a nice place to live but, in my opinion, the worst investment you could make. The sheer supply mitigates the population moving there; in fact, there may as well be negative population growth, given the over-supply of apartments, at the time of writing; it had a 22% vacancy rate. This phenomenon of some property developers diminishing the investment value in particular areas, by oversupply, is common.

Marketing companies seem to redefine the term 'artistic licence'. They typically have KPIs (targets to achieve in sales) and they generally make 5-6%, plus bonuses sometimes. They love selling to unsuspecting investors and the Asian market. The Asian market is susceptible to the tactics being used because they are accustomed to like small housing.

Small living spaces are common across Asia, but these types of housing developments are often ugly, monolithic, high-rise eyesores.

You must consider where the unit is, how many units there are in the building and in the project, how many there are in the immediate surrounds, the size of living, the cost of body corporate; the list goes on. Bear in mind that the more units there are, the more rival investors you are competing against for tenants, rent charged, and (when eventually you choose to sell your unit) how many other units there may be on the market at any given time.

Yes, some will be owner-occupied, but these statistics and figures will not be known by any one marketing company. There are often several marketing companies flogging these apartments/units, and obviously they do not know how many investors each marketing firm are selling to, versus owner-occupiers. The larger the percentage of investors the more it affects rental competition. But it does not matter how many are investors versus owner-occupiers; when it comes to selling, you are competing against everyone.

There are ways to reduce the risk with off the plan. These include only buying when there are just a few units or apartments on offer — no more than, let's say, fifty. There is no hard figure. Some people stick to developments with no more than twelve. Whatever you consider, remember that the more there are, the more you are competing with others.

So, to put it into context, the fact that units have only 10 % land value is a deterrent, there are a range of other issues that also negatively affect high-rise units. I have purchased units off the plan, but in a smaller development. This way they each have more land but, more importantly, they have less competition. They are more boutique and therefore unique, and naturally will attract more potential tenants and buyers.

I have heard some authors' comment that, in over fifty years, apartment buildings will be undesirable, or maybe even become a slum. These authors, however, rarely qualify their points, nor do they explain why. Additionally, they do not tend to drill down and bother separating high-rise from boutique — again, because of their vested interests in houses.

Townhouses are often off the plan as well. I think townhouses are necessary, and worth investing in. There are normally not many in the development, and they have more land (say roughly 20%-30% value, as a component of the overall purchase price.) They suit young families who may not be able to afford a house, and they suit soon-to-be retired, or retired, generations who want to downsize. Buying a townhouse can assist an investor afford a property closer in to the 10-20km radius of the city, at a lesser price than a house, and with more land content than units. Townhouses are bigger in size, and they're more appealing to people in many areas than units and houses.

Capital Growth versus Cash Flow Properties

Some people sell their concepts on the back of historical trends, and wield these trends as a crystal ball, stating that properties should double in value over the next 7-10 years. However, no one can predict the future, and there is speculation as to whether prices will double in some or many areas, compared to the past. They rely on this historical doubling to sell their strategies and properties. The reality is properties may not significantly increase in value straight away, or even in the first few years, so you cannot assume they will. Some authors say you should obtain a line of credit to fund repayments of your other mortgages. The problem is it is more debt, and it continues to affect servicing.

If you want to grow a good-sized portfolio, you need to have a balance of capital growth and cash flow properties.

Cash flow properties are not, necessarily, wealth creation properties. They do, however, provide greater income while you are growing your portfolio, thus allowing you to continue to borrow. If you only focus on capital growth properties you will exhaust your servicing capability, and it does not matter how much equity you have, you may not be able to access it.

You cannot just focus on cash flow properties either, as wealth creation stems from capital growth, not cash flow. Just focusing on cash flow also works against you by eating into all of your equity in your home and leaving you unable to purchase more properties (because you have run out of cash or equity.) Whilst you can borrow more money based on servicing, you may not have the deposit and costs accessible in cash, or equity, to put toward a new property. So, until banks start lending 100% of the purchase price, plus stamp duty (which will probably never happen), you must build a portfolio based on both cash flow and capital growth.

A friend of mine has built a portfolio of thirty-nine properties using these balanced strategies. Timing, as to when to use a cash flow strategy or a capital growth strategy, is one of the most important elements to a plan, reducing the risk of running out of servicing capacity or equity.

NRAS (applicable to any of the above)

The National Rental Affordability Scheme (NRAS), started by the Federal Government on 1 July 2008, was designed as a long-term response to the issue of rental affordability. The intent was to spur on the supply of 50,000 new affordable rental dwellings (the incentive can't be added to an existing dwelling), and reduce rental costs for low-to-moderate income households.

Incentives for investors

To encourage investors to buy these new rental dwellings, the Government offers guaranteed incentives that run for ten years. In return, investors must rent the dwellings to eligible approved tenants, at a rate at least 20% below market rent.

Currently, the incentive is $10,350 — a mix of State Government non-assessable income of $2,587, and Federal Government refundable tax credits/offsets or cash of $7,763.

Generally, investors receive the lower amount in September each year, and the Federal component in July/August, which may be then included in their tax returns.

Investors can have the normal benefits of negative gearing, but also the added benefit of positive cash flow (in terms of the tax offset.) But, if the incentive is provided to a not-for-profit approved participant, who then passes the value of the incentive through to an investor, there may be tax implications.

There are perceived disadvantages with NRAS, and several benefits. These may depend on a number of factors, such as where the property is, what it is, and who the tenant managers are.

Disadvantages: Tenant quality

The legislation sets out tenant eligibility. NRAS was designed to accommodate low-to-moderate income earners in critical industries — such as nurses, police, prison officers, fire-fighters, and teachers — whom cannot necessarily afford to live in the area in which they work.

In reality, many tenant managers are inserting tenants who are on welfare, or who are in the lower-socio-demographic of social housing tenants. NRAS is not a public housing initiative, hence the problem I have with some of the approved participants/tenant managers.

While there are maximum income bands (ranging from $45,956 for a single adult, to $109,264 for a couple and three children), the abuse of the spirit of NRAS (as some are calling it) is probably due to the fact there is no minimum income requirement for an eligible tenant. As long as they can pay the rent, many tenant managers could not care less.

Another major risk is that there can be a high concentration of NRAS-approved dwellings in the one area, due to the greed and irresponsibility of the developer mismanaging the situation, thereby compromising what could have been a good area for growth.

Issues about location

NRAS incentives are generally issued in agreement with State and Territory Governments for priority areas, with intensive criteria applied to the selection of the location. Amenities, schools, public transport, and employment are key drivers. They seek areas with a shortage of affordable dwellings in sought-after locations.

Investors are, in a way, riding on the back of the research the Government has already undertaken.

Others think these locations are rather less discriminate, and thus impact on capital growth.

Negative perceptions may be unrealistic

Some say they have not seen one of these properties sold for a profit yet.

But let's not forget the last few years have not been years of abundant market growth. Besides, although NRAS began in July 2008, it took two to three years to catch on, and not enough time has passed to make fair judgment. Additionally, NRAS investors would typically not sell them, given the incentives they receive.

There is simply not enough data to make this uninformed, scare-tactic statement. Some of the negativity is predicated on the self-interest of those making the comments.

Investors must take care to buy sensibly

An NRAS property looks the same as a non-NRAS property, so it should not affect the resale price. It can, however, depend on whether the developer, marketing company, or spruiker over-charged the buyer. This happens far too often (and not just on NRAS properties.)

Some negative reports make it sound impossible to sell an NRAS property without the NRAS licence attached. In most cases an investor can choose to sell with or without the NRAS overlay. However, this can be restricted by the purchasing arrangements the buyer originally entered into.

One of the biggest problems investors face is themselves — buying a property just because it is NRAS. The NRAS incentives can be good, but the need for adequate research remains.

Another hurdle is provided by accountants who lack the knowledge and skills to assist. Investors need an experienced accountant who understands property investment and NRAS.

Marketing companies and spruikers can be paid exorbitant fees to flog these properties to unsuspecting investors. Some developers are charging up to $20,000 more for providing an NRAS licence with the property. As a result, a 'black market' has materialised.

Valuers' have had issues with NRAS, due in part to the risk of high commissions being paid. This is due in part to these being 'off the plan' and/or 'house and land' (but this problem is not just with NRAS), and in part to their prejudices. Lenders have been hesitant to lend on NRAS properties for these reasons (and for reasons such as simply not understanding NRAS, or because of over-zealous credit and risk staff.)

The Government seems to be clamping down on the 'black market', and on the improper manner in which NRAS licences have been managed by some developers.

Good advice and research is essential

I cannot stress enough how important it is to seek advice, do your research, understand where and what the property is, understand who the consortium is (and the fees they charge, and the stipulations in their contracts), check the concentration of NRAS in the location and the type of tenant the consortium is dealing with, and examine the sale price and the commissions being paid.

NRAS is a good scheme but investors need to understand how it is being applied to the target property. It can provide excellent cash flow, and the potential for capital growth can be very good in many of these areas. Investors should carry out their own investigations and seek independent property and taxation advice.

Vendor Finance

Vendor finance is a form of private finance where the owner of a property (the vendor) agrees to sell the property under the provisions of a terms contract. The terms contract will outline all of the particulars of the sale agreement (including the purchase price and the period of time the payments will be made), as well as the payment amounts to complete the purchase of the property. In layman's terms, the owner of the property finances the purchaser.

These agreements are typically drawn up over a thirty year term, although the intention would be, in most instances, for the contract to be paid out much sooner than that when the purchaser is in a position to refinance the debt, by way of a conventional home/investment loan. This type of financing arrangement would appeal to a purchaser who, for whatever reason, can't qualify for a conventional loan at the time of purchase.

Structuring the agreement

The vendor and the purchaser agree on a sale price for the property. The purchaser should, and in most cases will, put down a deposit for the purchase, which will then be deducted from the sale price of the property. So let's say the sale price of the property is $250,000 and the purchaser puts down a deposit of $25,000. The remaining balance owed, under the terms contract, will be $225,000. It is on this remaining balance figure that the repayments, under the terms contract, will be calculated.

An interest rate will be agreed upon between the two parties, say 7%, and the repayments can be determined. On a thirty-year loan agreement, $225,000 at 7% means a weekly payment of $374.23. The purchaser is also responsible for paying the out-goings on the property

— like council and water rates, and insurance. These additional costs are then calculated and added to the weekly payment. For example they may total $40 per week, making the payment to the vendor $414.23.

The interest rate, under the terms contract, is most likely to change over the term of the agreement, just like it would under a conventional property loan arrangement. If it is a variable rate, which most are under these agreements, it will most likely be linked to any changes by the reserve bank, or if the vendor has a mortgage over the property it may be linked to any changes in that interest rate. Fixed rates can be agreed to under a terms contract, but like conventional fixed rate property loans, they can be subject to break costs if the loan is paid out, or greatly reduced, during the fixed-rate term.

Whilst under a terms contract agreement, the title of the property remains in the vendor's name. This will also mean that the council and water rates, as well as insurance, will also be in the vendors name: paid by the vendor, and recouped each week via the weekly payment, under the terms contract agreement. Title to the property transfers to the purchaser when final payment *and* stamp duty is paid, to complete the property transfer.

The purchaser will also be responsible for any other costs that arise in relation to the property, like maintenance and repairs. This is because rights to the ownership of the property belong to the purchaser — from the date and signing of the terms contract — meaning the purchaser is entitled to all future capital growth in the property, and is therefore responsible for all costs associated with the property, just like any property owner.

Vendors Obligations

As the vendor is providing finance, the vendor will need to comply with any legislative requirements for a finance provider. These will include (but are not limited to):

- Ensuring the finance is not unsuitable to the purchaser
- Making sure the council and water rates, as well as insurance, are paid and up-to-date
- Confirming and verifying the borrowers can meet their financial obligation, under the terms contract agreement
- Ensuring the vendor provide regular loan statements to the purchaser
- Meeting its financial obligations — if there is a mortgage on the property
- Ensuring there are no changes to any mortgage over the property, after the terms contract agreement has been signed, including (but not limited to) increasing the debt or refinancing
- Ensuring the property is not cross-collateralised with any other properties
- Having a dispute resolution mechanism in place
- Ensuring proper process is followed, and appropriate action is taken if the purchaser falls into arrears, or they develop poor conduct on the loan facility.

I would just like to elaborate a little further on the point about ensuring the finance is not unsuitable to the purchaser. It is critical that the vendor takes appropriate steps to understand the purchaser's objectives, and assess whether entering into a terms contract will, in fact, address and meet those objectives. By entering into the agreement, is the purchaser likely to be able to complete the agreement at some point in the future? Is their income sufficient to meet their loan repayment commitments? Are there any foreseeable changes that may affect their capacity to meet their obligations under the agreement? If all reasonable steps have been taken to satisfy these points, then a vendor terms contract can be considered as a viable option for the purchaser to buy a home.

Benefits for the Vendor

Offering a property for sale under a terms contract can have many benefits to a vendor, particularly for vendors where the property is an investment. It is a great way for an investor to receive more income from the property, than would normally be achieved if the property was rented out. This additional income will certainly mean this investment is making money each year, which can be used as a supplementary income for the vendor, or used to boost the overall cash flow of the vendor's property investment portfolio.

This additional cash flow is a very powerful element for investors wanting to expand their property portfolio. When applying for finance to purchase a property, you need to demonstrate to the lender that you have enough income to service the debt you are requesting. Having property/properties where you have significant surplus income, over and above all costs, means you have additional income that you can evidence to demonstrate your capacity to take on more debt. In most instances, having a terms contract in place will increase your borrowing capacity, so the more of these you have in your portfolio, (potentially) the more property you can buy.

You will also have an occupant of the property, who is planning on staying there for an extended period of time, providing the vendor with more revenue certainty. The occupant will also be more likely to take care of the property, and it is also very common for the purchaser to make improvements to the property. After all, they are purchasing it.

In some instances, under a terms contract, the purchaser will not complete the contract and may request to be released from the contract. This can have huge benefits for the vendor. The vendor was collecting substantial income during the time the agreement was in place, and now that the purchaser has been released from the contract the vendor is again the only person with an interest in the property, and is therefore entitled to all future capital growth in the property (from the date of the release letter being signed.) The vendor will be obligated, though, to pay the outgoing purchaser any equity they have built up in the property during the time the terms contract was in place.

Having just outlined the benefits to the vendor, assuming the purchaser does not request a release from the contract and does go on to complete the purchase, the vendor has traded the additional income for not receiving any capital growth in the property over and above the agreed sale price. It certainly doesn't detract from the benefits that can be gained from the terms contract, but it does highlight that this arrangement is an income generating strategy, and a far less capital appreciation strategy.

Benefits for the purchaser

As with the vendor, the purchaser gains many benefits by purchasing a property under a terms contract. It's great for purchasers who have a small deposit, which wouldn't meet the minimum amount required if applying for a loan through a conventional mortgage provider. This enables purchasers, in this position, to enter the property market sooner than they otherwise could have.

Vendors will also consider purchasers that may have a less than perfect credit history, which, again, can be a barrier to obtaining finance the conventional way. This by no means suggests that vendors will provide this opportunity to everyone, but a personalised solution can be assessed, based on the credit history of the purchaser.

Purchasers that have varied income streams can also be considered as suitable purchasers under terms contracts. This can include people starting a new job, changing industries, starting a business, reliant on commission or bonuses, or self-employed people who don't have their financial records up-to-date. Purchasers, in these categories, can often be overlooked in the conventional financing arena as unsuitable borrowers. Diligent assessment will need to be undertaken for people in these categories, but solutions can often be found to assist purchasers who find themselves in this position.

The purchaser really does have control over the property, which provides comfort and certainty. Changes and improvements to the property can and often are undertaken, which can help increase the rate at which equity is building in the property. The purchaser can also sell the property on the open market, or negotiate with the vendor to pay them out their equity, should their circumstances change and they need to move on.

Interest rates and fees that may apply to terms contracts are often in line with (if not more competitive than) a non-conforming lender that provides finance solutions to purchasers who fall into some of the categories I mentioned earlier. Terms contracts really are a genuine alternative for purchasers seeking a solution to enter the property market.

The Risks

Although vendor finance really is a win/win for both parties, like all investments/opportunities, there are risks that need to be understood and considered before either party enters into an agreement. The vendor needs to ensure they are compliant with their obligations under the agreement, and complete their due diligence on the purchaser to ensure they are credit-worthy applicants (who can fulfil their obligations under the agreement as well.) The vendor can face significant disruption, to the performance of the terms contract if the purchaser fails to meet their obligation, and it can take time and financial resources to bring the purchaser back in line, or move them on.

From the purchaser's position, they need to be dealing with a credible vendor who agrees to fair and reasonable terms in the agreement; particularly with the sale price, interest rate, and fees, to ensure there is real opportunity for the purchaser to complete the contract at some point in the future. The vendor also needs to meet their obligation under the agreement and, in particular, meet their financial commitments to the property outgoings and any mortgage that may be on the property.

Seeking the right professional advice is critical for both parties to ensure the agreement is compliant in every way, and that it meets the needs of both the vendor and purchaser. Risk shouldn't be a barrier to either party entering into a terms contract agreement: they just need to be understood, and appropriate action taken to mitigate and minimise them.

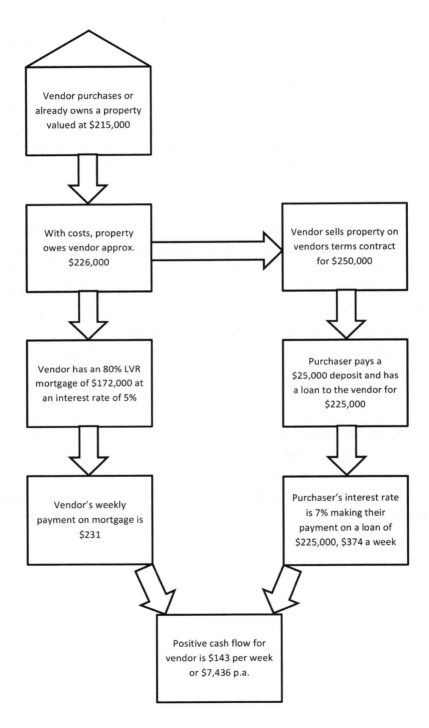

Vendor purchases or already owns a property valued at $215,000

With costs, property owes vendor approx. $226,000

Vendor sells property on vendors terms contract for $250,000

Vendor has an 80% LVR mortgage of $172,000 at an interest rate of 5%

Purchaser pays a $25,000 deposit and has a loan to the vendor for $225,000

Vendor's weekly payment on mortgage is $231

Purchaser's interest rate is 7% making their payment on a loan of $225,000, $374 a week

Positive cash flow for vendor is $143 per week or $7,436 p.a.

Case Study

'Starting out as a property investor, I was very much aware of the importance of cash flow. I knew that it would be an integral part of my investment strategy to build and maintain a strong cash flow position. It was a strong focus of mine from the outset, particularly given my financial position at the time I was building my portfolio — with limited capital and a very modest income.

'My personal property investment strategy was quite heavily weighted on purchasing properties that were generating good income, in part given my personal circumstances, but also because it just made a lot of sense to me to purchase assets that produced income, over and above the costs associated with holding that asset. This wasn't always achievable with the properties I was buying, and I was finding I needed to contribute funds to the portfolio to support it on a monthly basis.

'Despite having some properties that were making money each month, albeit only by a handfull of dollars, it only took some small unanticipated expenses to enter into negative cash flow territory. I was also finding the more properties I was buying, the more exaggerated the issue became. If I was going to continue to grow and expand my property portfolio, I needed to find a solid cash flow solution that would turn this situation around.

'I was introduced to vendor financing, in around 2006, and became very interested in the concept immediately. I tried to find out as much as I could about how it worked, and search for people who could help me implement it. My initial experiences were less than ideal, and the people I entrusted to help me had a lot of fundamental issues with their implementation of the strategy. A key aspect to a successful terms contract agreement is to have a credible purchaser, and this was the area in which the people I engaged to help got it horribly wrong.

'As the first three properties I purchased (specifically to use a terms contract strategy on) slowly started to unravel, it became clear to me that the purchasers I had been advised to sell my properties to were unsuitable for this type of transaction. Failings in two key areas became apparent: lack of deposit put down by the purchaser, as well as very unstable employment history (in conjunction with the use of Government benefits to demonstrate capacity to service debt.) Looking back now, those first three attempts at making this strategy work were destined to fail from the outset.

'Believing in the concept, and accepting my failed attempts to make this strategy work were due to getting the fundamentals wrong, I set out to better educate myself and find the right people to help me execute this correctly. It wasn't long before I was surrounded by experienced people who were having success with the strategy. With their help and guidance, I was able to turn a quite unsuccessful moment in my property investing journey into a very successful and important one, for my growth going forward.

'At one point, I had just over ten of these deals in place, making anywhere from $600-$1000 a month positive cash flow, after all expenses. This couldn't have come at a better time as, unbeknown to me at the time, we were heading for the GFC and interest rates were rising, putting my portfolio under the most extreme cash flow pressure I had experienced. This surplus cash flow I had created not only ensured I survived the GFC well, but strengthened my portfolio to enable me to expand it at the rate I wanted to.

'Seven years on, from when I first came across the terms contract concept, I am now able to reflect back on how this strategy has played out, and how the agreements reach a conclusion. I've had a number of purchasers fall behind with their financial obligations (of the agreement) and I have been required to move them on from the property. On the surface this *may not appear to be a desired outcome, but it's actually not as bad as it sounds. Some people will fall behind. It happens on conventional contracts as well, and they need to take responsibility for that situation. In this instance, the purchaser moves out of the property and no longer has any entitlement to the property. If there is equity that has been built up over the time the purchaser has been there, then that is theirs, and as the vendor I am obligated, and do, pay that to them. I can then enter into another terms contract agreement, rent the property out, or sell it.*

'In my experience, most purchasers will meet their obligations under the agreement, and the terms contract works well for both parties. Most of the terms contracts I have entered into are still in place, and are working well for both myself and the purchaser. The longest has been going for around five years and, I'd say, it won't be many more years now before there has been adequate growth in the properties, for the purchasers to then seriously consider refinancing and completing the agreement. I look forward to these coming to successful conclusions, where both parties have achieved their objectives and benefitted accordingly.

'Deciding on what to do with a property, when I take back full control of it, will depend on what my property portfolio needs at the time. If it needs additional cash flow then I will on-sell it again, on a terms contract. If the cash flow position of the portfolio is sound, then I will most likely rent the property out — which really is a fabulous outcome for the vendor/investor. If my portfolio is in this strong cash flow position, I will be able to change strategy with the property, and benefit from the capital growth in the future.

'For me personally, terms contracts played a significant role in allowing me to build a reasonably large property portfolio, and manage the cash flow in a way that required very little financial input from me. I made this very strategic decision, as I didn't want to be a slave to my investments, and truly wanted them to work for me. For some, terms

contracts are the primary investment strategy delivering great cash flow, which results in financial flexibility by providing an alternative to working a regular job. For me, it added strength and diversity to my portfolio and, looking back now, even after a rocky start, was one of the best decisions that I would repeat again if starting over.'
— **Garry Harvey**

Defence Housing

You are buying a property, like any other investment property, with possibly the same potential for growth, roughly the same yield, and maybe a tad less rent than something comparable. The military are not always based in areas of growth, so it is not considered wise to purchase defence housing purely based on it being defence housing.

You need to make sure all the due diligence and research into capital growth potential has been carried out. The difference is you have the luxury of effectively guaranteed rent, although it is referred to, by the Defence Housing Association (DHA), as 'reliable rent with zero vacancy rate risk' and 'certainty for the entire term of the lease'. The period is for six, nine, or twelve years, with the option to extend for a period of time.

You pay higher than normal management fees, which include managing the property, general service and repairs, emergency repairs, annual valuation to adjust the rent to market rent, and a restoration service for the end of the lease period (re-carpet for example, and other overhauls.)

The price may be higher than the same dwelling, in the same area, due to the requirement to follow the procedures and protocols of inclusions, and so forth, which could over-capitalise the price for the area.

Common mistakes that investors make:

- Having a principle and interest loan (P/I) rather than interest only (I/O) on your investment property loan. Investment debt is tax deductable debt. Why reduce good debt (i.e. debt that saves you money (tax) that currently goes to the Government?)
- Having a line of credit (LOC) carries with it some problematic tax consequences as well. Having an offset account is more beneficial. You can be your own bank. In other words you can access the redraw (monies you have accumulated in the offset account, known as redraw of monies you have saved), or monies provided by a previous loan application.
- Ownership in the name of the person with the lower income. It is the ownership split on title that determines the tax benefit apportionment, rather than who is on the loan.
- Buying a one million dollar property when you are reaching beyond your means. This is okay if you have plenty of money, but if it has 'maxed' out your borrowing capacity, or if it will cause pressure on your lifestyle, then do not do it. Borrowing under 500k (unless it is a dual occupancy property) is generally considered better as there are more buyers at a lower level, you are spreading your risk by not putting all your buying power in the one property, and more people can afford this level. If the property is vacant, there is less debt you have to service — i.e. 2 x $500k properties will earn more than 1 x $1million property usually, and if one is vacant, the other will probably have a tenant. Therefore, you reduce your exposure to the same debt that you would be exposed to, if you borrowed for a $1million property.
- Lack of research by ending up on busy roads, near power lines, industrial areas, or in a social welfare-housing neighbourhood.
- Not commissioning a quantity surveyor to undertake a depreciation schedule.
- Managing land tax exposure.

- Buying specifically in the state you live in, thinking your property is safer simply because you live there.
- Not treating the investment as a business.
- Investors fail if they sell their property to purchase a business, pay school fees, or buy elsewhere but have not given the property enough time to increase in value. Make sure you don't forget about property cycles.
- Property is a long-term process. Most experts agree with this if the property is a 'buy and hold' property for a time-poor investor, rather than a subdivision or active investor strategy. Many people forget this.
- Forgetting to take out landlord insurance (and other necessary insurances such as building insurance), if there is no body corporate in place.
- Spending too much for the area you buy in, so you're not just overcapitalising on repairs and additions/inclusions, but also paying too much for the property.
- 'Including a 'subject to finance' clause in the purchase contract, but forgetting to include a 'due diligence' clause as well.'
- Forgetting to factor in all costs: rates, insurance, agent fees, maintenance allowance, and water.
- Forgetting to factor in stamp duty, purchasing or selling costs, and/or capital gains tax. If people thought about exit costs, just as much as they do entry costs, they would possibly reconsider selling.
- Waiting for the perfect property, and then waking up to find you're sixty-five, and have done nothing.
- Reducing your investment loan before paying off your home loan.
- Stopping at one or two properties. Most people feel content doing nothing, because doing nothing involves no risk to most people. Consequently they feel safer in their bubble.
- Not knowing your borrowing capacity.
- Using emotion.
- Not treating this like a business.

- Not planning ahead for the third property.
- Doing it yourself.
- Buying in a 'one horse town'.
- Listening to backyard experts (friends and family) who all have an opinion.

Chapter 7

Best Property Management ... TIP 6

You may not be aware of this but a larger number of houses are rented (leased) than actually bought (purchased).

Rental or *leased* properties come under the banner of the following:

1. Commercial properties for lease — offices, shops and shopping centres, for example
2. Industrial properties for lease — factories and warehouses
3. Residential properties — houses, flats, apartments, and holiday letting.

Commercial and industrial property leasing is beyond the scope of this book and therefore will not be discussed here. Instead the focus will be on residential leasing, which (for the most part) is a large division within most real estate agencies. Smaller real estate agencies may have a hundred or so rental properties, whilst larger agencies can have in excess of several thousand properties.

From an agent's perspective, the rental market offers a continued source of income. This is independent of the actual selling market (i.e. the properties that are for sale.) Therefore potential buyers of a real estate business take this into account above the actual selling market.

What constitutes a real estate rental division

The rental division usually consists of a rental manager and one or more assistants depending on the number of rentals. Their role is to manage the day-to-day operations of the department, including:

- Advertising any vacancies
- Interviewing potential tenants
- Drawing up leases for successful applicants
- Preparing condition reports on the property
- Maintaining the property (for instance, ensuring all appliances are in working order, and attending to minor repairs)
- Collecting rental monies from occupants
- Following up on any complaints and disputes, including attending to required legalities and attending the tribunal if required
- Attending property inspections (which are usually every six months.)

It is important that those working within a rental division should have a good working knowledge of the Residential Tenancies Act to ensure a comprehensive understanding of situations that *may* potentially arise or that *do* actually arise. Not all do though and you must be choosy with the rental agent you appoint.

Finding the right tenant

One of the problems agents have to deal with is finding a suitable tenant for a particular property. This entails the following:

- Reference checks
- Ascertaining whether the tenant has a regular job or at least the capacity to afford and pay the rental price being asked
- If there are multiple applications for a property, the agent has the

right to choose the applicant that is most suitable. If there is only one applicant and the agent feels that this particular applicant is not suitable, then the applicant will not progress to the next stage. It is important to mention here that in this scenario there is a risk that the agent could potentially be accused of discrimination. Unfortunately these types of tenants are often street cunning, and more often than not, aware of the anti-discrimination act (often aided and abetted by lawyers according to a number of agents.) A good agent will ensure that he/she has the necessary diplomatic skills to avoid this scenario.

Dealing successfully with rentals does require agents to have the knowledge, expertise, and systems in place to ensure that the property is managed properly.

When Things Go Wrong (And They DO!)

Whilst there have been horror stories of 'trashed' properties and months of unpaid rent, it is fortunately comparatively rare. Often these situations occur when the landlord tries to deal directly with the tenant without following the due process. In this scenario, when things go wrong, the landlord is left to deal with the aftermath and has no back-up.

Agents should be chosen carefully after some background research to avoid settling for someone that is somewhat remiss about the whole process. If an agent is involved and their actions are found to be negligent or at fault then at least there are some avenues for compensation.

On the flip side there have been some landlords who take advantage of a desperate tenant (e.g. students, migrants, and — sometimes — illegal immigrants.) These types of landlords need the full weight of the law to come down on them. On a more positive note, the majority of landlords are normal people who have one or more rental properties and require them to be run properly in order to pay the due mortgage.

What to Look For in an Agent

When choosing a rental agent, always look for:

- A well-established company with a good sales team and well established rental division
- Ensure the commission paid is well spent. This is generally 7% plus GST for their management fee to collect rent and one to two weeks' rent for leasing.

From time to time a landlord will upgrade or add to his/her portfolio. In this instance the landlord will often look to the agent to sell the unwanted property. If keeping the property, they can try to negotiate a lower management fee (when having multiple properties managed by the same agent.) This ensures an ongoing and mutually beneficial relationship with the agent.

Agents managing properties often ask for references, usually from previous landlords or agents. Often these references are written as an inducement to leave rather than being a genuine reference, which can negatively impact on the applicant who, in actual fact, is a good tenant. A good agent will check the references via a follow up phone call to the agent or landlord, and also check that the applicant does have a regular job, time of tenure etc. In this instance a good agent will also call upon further references such as those from a central credit agency that will show up any bad debts or adverse credit history relating to the applicant.

Background on the tenant should include: gaps in rental history, employment, salary, references etc. An ideal tenant is renting through a real estate agent and has rented through a real estate agent previously.

The main reason for this is because a solid rental history can be obtained from the previous agent, whilst a tenant ledger can also be requested, which often re-affirms what the managing agent has told the new agent. If the tenant is renting privately, ownership searches are completed on the property to ensure the specified owner is indeed the owner; if a person owns their own home a good manager will ask for a rates notice as proof of ownership and generally speak to their sales agent for details.

Dates this person has been in the property are checked to ensure there are no gaps; if there are gaps the case is more often than not that this person is not specifying the details for a reason and this casts doubt over the honesty of the person. Once their residential details are confirmed, the focus is then on their income. If they are self-employed, an ABN check is done, and contact made with their accountant to request end of financial year summaries.

If a person is working for a company, a good agent will do a web search on the company and do ABN searches to ensure they are a legitimate company. Mobile numbers should not be called for references — only landline and business numbers should be confirmed. Furthermore, only head members of staff should be spoken to (i.e. managers or directors) to ensure the applicant's friend is not being spoken to.

If a person is not employed and is receiving Centrelink benefits, a Centrelink statement and a bank statement would be asked for to ensure the income coming in is sustainable and sufficient to accommodate for rent and everyday living expenses. Once these thorough checks are completed, all applications will go to you, the landlord, to make the ultimate decision, accompanied with recommendations. A bad rental agent will probably be too lazy to provide recommendations (including feedback on quality of references, etc., which would allow the landlord to make an informed decision.)

The National Tenancy Database provides considerable risk assessment information on tenants and is another way to investigate suitability of a prospective tenant and conduct a tenant evaluation.

Common mistakes made by a landlord when selecting a managing agent

Many landlords tend to focus on fees and 'fee shop' to find the cheapest agent. You will often find with cheap fees comes poor service and poor communication. You ideally want an agent that is flexible on fees yet willing to maintain the integrity of their department.

You want to ensure you are going with a brand name company; the main reason being they are reputable, reviews can be looked up online, and they are backed by a corporate entity. However, the biggest brand is not necessarily the best as you may receive poor service due to their size, or be handed back and forth between property managers. What you're looking for is a firm that is small enough to offer personalised service, however big enough that they have a brand identity to protect.

When selecting an agent they will provide you with their fees. If they sound too good to be true, they normally are. Ensure that all of their fees are laid out to you from the beginning, and ensure there are no 'hidden extras'. A good managing agent will specify every fee including the ones that may come up during a tenancy, such as lease renewal or VCAT attendance (the latter may never come up, but it is better to know anyway.)

Ensure that the team you are dealing with has the knowledge and experience that your property deserves. Be confident with the people you have given your property to, and have trust that they will look after the property as if it was their own.

Misconceptions landlords can have

Many landlords expect that the tenant will always pay the rent on time, and expect the money in their account for payment of their mortgage. This is unrealistic and landlords should have the equivalent of one month's rent extra in their account to cover any unforeseen problems with the tenant paying their rent (i.e. loss of job, admittance to hospital, etc.)

Many landlords that manage their own properties have a lack of knowledge regarding tenant's rights, landlord rights, and how to go about addressing issues within the tenancy. A perfect example could be the process of removing a tenant who has not paid their rent, or has done something that allows them to be removed, and what exactly these things are that could constitute removal.

A good managing agent will constantly follow up with the tenant and update the landlord. When a tenant falls fifteen days in arrears a notice to evict can and will be served; this lets the tenant know there is no tolerance for late payments. The tenant then has three business days to make payment that will get them out of the fifteen-day bracket. Should they not make payment an application to VCAT can be made for possession, rent, and, in some cases, the bond, if the arrears are equivalent to the bond amount.

Other issues that can result in termination of tenancy include consecutive breaches relating to damage, unclean premises, and disturbance of the peace. When issuing a breach, and ultimately ending a tenancy based on these breaches, the damage or uncleanliness must be to the extent that warrants removal of the tenant (i.e. severe damage to walls, floors, fittings and fixtures, broken windows, damage that may leave the property unsafe, etc.) Another major breach is uncleanliness to the point where there is a large odour to the premises that will cost hundreds of dollars to remove.

Process you undertake if damage occurs in a property and how the property manager goes about rectifying the problem

The process taken, if damage is noted at a routine inspection or is brought to the attention of the agent, is reinspected within fourteen days. A breach warning for any problems or damage is issued first, explaining to the tenant their rights and responsibilities and explaining the time frame for the repair to be carried out. Once the re-inspection is completed, if the damage is not repaired and in a tradesman like manner, a formal breach of duty notice is served (a notice of repair can also be served at this time.) The difference between a breach and a notice of repair is that a breach is like a bad report and notice against their names, whereas a notice to repair is simply advising them that the work must be completed within fourteen days or the agent can have the work carried out at the tenants expense.

The property can be re-inspected every fourteen days and if damage is not repaired the process calls for three consecutive breaches. Once this occurs a notice to vacate can then be served for consecutive breaches. It is often found that after the first or second breach the issue is completed and resolved.

Many landlords are actually accepting of pets; it is only a small portion of landlords who are concerned, and it is normally only a few tenants that ruin it for everyone else. It is the same for anything really. It only takes a few to become the reason for new legislation, compliance, rules, etc. When a person has a pet, the previous landlord or agent is contacted to confirm what this pet was like: was there any damage, bad odours, etc.? This generally demonstrates how the tenant will look after the property with the pet in place. If the pet has a bad reference it is wise to not proceed with the tenant.

Allowing pets can increase how many potential tenants may be interested in applying to move in. For any person that has a pet in a property, an additional animal clause is added to the contract. The clause states that any damage caused by the pet must be rectified by the tenant, and that the landlord can be indemnified for cost. It also states that the property must be deodorized and carpets steam cleaned upon the tenant vacating.

One potential issue is the animals not going outside to do their business. This can lead to stains going all the way down to the underlay: a problem steam cleaning does not remove, but simply acts as a band aid.

All but one of my properties has a clause in the contract stipulating no pets; the one with the pet is one of the best tenants I have had: a single older lady who needs some company. Most of the flooring is tiles, which definitely helps, and it is an indoor dog. Many people may think an outdoor dog is better if you consider having pets but often the owners may let the dog inside and obviously the dog is not necessarily house trained, and it also brings in the outside.

An indoor dog is more likely to be house trained. Some pet owners may offer to pay a bit of extra rent knowing that it is difficult to rent with an animal.

Consider negotiating to have an extra bond paid from the tenant for the pet. There is already a bond paid anyway.

Allowing a pet may retain the tenant longer given the tenant will find it difficult to go elsewhere. You could have a lower vacancy or find a tenant to move in straight away.

I have only had one property where it was vacant for several weeks, and upon reflection, having a pet friendly policy may have helped, but then again, the real problem was the uselessness of the rental agent.

It does also depend on the property. Many body corporates do not allow pets.

Things a landlord could do to an existing property to make it rent easier

There are some basic tips to help make a property more attractive for prospective tenants:

1. Ensure the property is clean and well presented. It may sound basic but it will help promote a tenant that will look after the property and will be house proud and helps prospective tenants visualise themselves in the property.
2. Remove any personal photographs from the walls. Again, this will help the prospective tenant feel more comfortable.
3. A property that is freshly painted presents well and is easier to maintain and is ideal for prospective tenants.
4. Ensure all appliances and fittings are in good working order and all manuals provided to assist with easy usage.
5. Tidy lawns and gardens, and remove weeds. This, once again, promotes for a tenant that will look after the gardens thereafter, and ensures the property will also look neat and tidy for inspections.

Why it is not allowed to forbid a tenant from smoking on the property, but it *is* possible to prevent them from smoking inside

Unfortunately you are not allowed to stop someone from smoking merely on the premises, as they are allowed quiet enjoyment of their property and we cannot discriminate against tenants who do smoke. However, you are allowed to prevent them smoking inside and stipulate that it is not allowed, as smoking inside premises can cause damage and is something that can lead to a breach. It is similar to an agent not being able to stipulate how a tenant pays the rent, but they can stipulate that arrears are not tolerated.

Check out my interview with Jenny Newman, a Property Manager

http://www.austpag.com.au/premium-content

Property Inspections

Pre-Purchase Building Inspections and Pest Inspection

It is important to be aware that borrowing money for a property is a big commitment! Below are some points for consideration:

- Due diligence is vital when purchasing a property (in other words doing your research and knowing what you are committing to.)
- Emotions may be running high even if the property is an investment, and especially if it is a first time purchase.
- Opportunity to view the property may be difficult. For example, you may not have full access to the roof space or floor level below.
- Timing may be restricted with respect to available inspection times. For instance, you may have only half an hour. Some properties may not even be built yet, in which case plans are all you have to go by.
- Workmanship needs careful consideration, some of which you may not have expertise in and may need to acquire someone who does. Often there are common issues with new and old property.
- Often there may be a sense of urgency that impedes on the time

needed for the careful consideration of whether the property is right for you. This may include an impending auction date or simply other interested parties in the property.

- Don't let presentation of a property distract you from looking for underlying defects.
- Some defects may be of a minor nature but if left unattended could result in costly and timely repairs in the future.

An Independent Building Inspection is Not Only the Smart Thing to do, it is Vitally Important

- A report will document any potential problem or defect and offer a possible solution. Consider a leaking shower recess for example. By using a moisture meter around the shower recess a leak can be detected and fixed with an application of a flexible silicone sealant to overcome the problem and avoid further damage.
- The report will identify whether any defects are a major or minor defect, and whether in fact they pose a safety issue.
- A report will be a handy reference if you do purchase the property; especially if future maintenance is required.

A pest inspection is also advisable for the following reasons:

- To identify if there are any pests present, in particular, termites
- If conditions are the sort of environment that pests would like.

Regardless of the age of the house, an independent inspection can be invaluable.

If you were building a new home would you know if you were getting all you paid for?

A Building Inspection is invaluable

- Houses can be very complex with respect to the many varying components and strict regulations that need to be adhered to in order to ascertain a workable, safe, and sound property.
- You may have outlaid expenses for plans, engineering, soil testing applications, and energy reports, just to name a few. Make sure you get full advantage!
- It is important that your builder adheres to any details on the plans, as far as specifications, recommendations in engineering calculations, and the energy report.
- An independent inspection can include review of your documentation to see that it has been completed correctly and accurately.
- Early detection of problems is vital to allow for fixing the issue before the building process continues.
- Progress stage inspections will ensure each progress payment is paid only when all works have been completed.
- All new homes have a seven-year guarantee period; however, the warranty for some components of new homes diminishes over time. A report can identify which items are still covered at any time during the subsequent seven-year period.

It is important to be aware that even though you may be using these big firms (that advertise on TV, etc.), for building your investment property, most of them (if not possibly all of them) outsource the work to different tradesmen. Many tradesmen are excellent; some are useless and cut corners in order to achieve their goal of 'quantity, not necessarily quality'.

Check out my interview with Ian Donaldson, a property inspector.

http://www.austpag.com.au/premium-content

Chapter 8

Money Talks ... TIP 7

I believe our schools should be doing more to educate students on the reality of life, financial literacy, and the importance of research and responsibility. I once ran seminars for mortgage brokers, which included a presentation that could be given to Year 11 and 12 students, on the importance of paying bills on time. Often teenagers do not care, nor do they understand this responsibility. Many people applying for a loan do not understand the detriment of having blemishes on their credit file.

Interest rates are not the be all and end all — it is the availability of money that influences peoples' borrowing habits and confidence.

Different Loans

Fixed-rate and Variable-rate Loan

Your repayments will not change during this a fixed-rate period. Many people have complained about break costs when leaving their lender, or wanting to reduce their interest rate. Let's not get confused between break costs and breaking a fixed-rate term. Break costs were abolished in July 2011, so lenders cannot charge deferred establishment fees/ mortgage discharge fees on loans entered into after that date. This used to be %, based on how long the individual has been with the lender. Administration fees still apply though when discharging. If a person attempts to exit a fixed-rate loan, they will usually pay heavily to do so — and this is quite fair.

Individuals obtaining fixed-rate loans want to have their repayments remain unchanged for a period, maybe because the rate they obtained was good, or maybe they just want the comfort of knowing what they have to pay every month. This is a contract. You sign the agreement. You cannot break your agreement and decide that you don't like it anymore (especially just because interest rates are going down further.) Fixed rates are good if variable rates are increasing, but are not good if variable rates are coming down. You are gambling when choosing between fixed-rates and variable rates, and it is a gamble you need to live with if it is a fixed-rate you want. If it's a variable rate you want then you can always fix it later.

Variable rates are affected by how greedy the lender is. They may have a front end rate and a back end rate (i.e. if you are already a client, the rate on your loan may not be as low as the rate the lenders offers to new client.) Lenders change the rate independent of the RBA in regards to the amount, more so than the timing.

Brokers cannot advise as to whether you should fix your rate and it is unfair for them to be expected to. I know some consumers try to avoid taking responsibility for their actions and want someone else to make their decision for them, meaning they have someone to blame if it does not work out. Unfortunately for that type of individual, they must make their own decisions. This decision can be made easier though, with a good broker. A good broker will have an understanding of the market, the economy, and what the media and different economists are saying. The broker will share that knowledge with their client to then help the client make a more informed decision.

Bridging Finance

This type of finance is useful if you find a new house you wish to buy, but have not yet sold your current property. It enables you to borrow for the new property, even though you may not normally have been able to afford the debt on both properties at the same time. Lenders who provide bridging finance can allow servicing to be based on the end debt (i.e. the debt calculated assuming the current property you wish to sell is sold.) They allow up to six months for existing dwellings, or twelve months for construction, for no repayments to be made on any of the debt, in some cases. The interest on the total debt of both properties is added to the loan, because you've still borrowed all that debt, but the lender allows you a repayment 'holiday' by adding the interest to the loan. There are loan-to-value/debt against equity (LVR) limits that can be inclusive of the capitalised interest and any applicable loan mortgage insurance (LMI). The LVR can be up to 85%.

The risk with bridging finance is that you may be unable to sell the property you wish to sell in the allotted time frame (of either six or twelve months) and at that point you must commence making repayments on the entire debt. If you cannot afford to, it's too bad! You risk repossession and losing both properties.

Split Loans

When a split loan is taken, the total loan amount is split into two or more smaller loans. Each split can be either a fixed rate or variable rate (that is if the lender offers fixed rates.) Some lenders allow you to name each split. If you're buying with a friend, and wish to keep payments and responsibilities separate, then a split can help. Bear in mind that, in almost every instance, you will be jointly and severally liable for the entire debt — even though you may be only receiving part of the rent.

100% Offset versus Redraw

An offset account is a separate account linked to the loan, with the primary purpose being to help reduce interest repayments on the loan. It offsets the loan principle. Interest is calculated on the principle amount of the loan, less any monies you have saved in the offset account. You may also redraw any monies saved in this account. Redraw accounts are different as they often tend to refer to the loan itself, and the ability to put extra monies directly into the loan, and being able to redraw those monies. Sometimes a minimum amount is required to be taken out when wanting access to your money/ redraw able figure. There may be a charge to withdraw it, and it may not offset the loan amount beyond the initial month it is paid into the loan.

Principle & Interest versus Interest Only Loans

Principle and interest loans have higher repayments than interest only loans, as some of the repayment is going toward reducing the loan principle over, typically, a thirty-year period. Some lenders offer up to a forty-year period. Lenders may offer the option of a shorter repayment term, particularly if you are over sixty years old. In the early years of the term of the loan, the majority of the repayment is interest, and only a small amount is principle. It is often better to have fortnightly repayments, rather than monthly, due to the fact that the lenders compound the interest every day — in other words, they charge interest not only on the loan amount, but also on the interest charged on the loan amount 'every day', until the repayment comes out. So, if you pay fortnightly, the compound interest has not compounded as much on the interest accumulated so far, given that when you make a payment the compound interest commences again the next day.

Over time, the principle component of the repayment starts to reduce the principle. One of the main reasons the first several years of repayments consist mainly of interest (as a greater component of the repayment), is due to the fact the bank is not a 'not-for-profit organisation'. They are a business. Banks are not in the business of lending you money. They are in the business of making money from you, by lending you money and, given the average time a person remains with their lender is 3.5 years, it makes sense that the lenders want to make as much money as possible from you. Every time you refinance you start the thirty-year loan term all over again, effectively going backwards.

Valuations

Some lenders require a valuer to go to the property, whilst others just use a software program; this program is designed to provide an approximate value without someone visiting the property. Occasionally a valuation is not required; again, it is very useful to use a broker to compare choices of lender for you.

These involve looking into comparable sales for lending purposes — not what the property will sell for. Some lenders allow you to choose the valuer.

Some sales firms mislead you by saying it is important to get a copy of the valuation; they wield this as yet another tool to convince you to use their vertically-integrated 'rip off' of a model and overpriced funding. If the valuation comes in okay, then everyone is happy anyway; if it does not, receiving a valuation is irrelevant. Sometimes it can be important to get a copy of the comparable sales used, then find your own, and provide this information back to the funder, in order to attempt to get the valuer to change his mind. Often valuers have their pride to protect, so it can be seldom they will admit they are wrong. It does happen though, and I have had a few valuations increased. Even if you cannot obtain a list of the comparable sales the valuer has used, you can still look for others that you believe support the value of your property.

Most lenders order their valuation through a third party. This is effectively a medium through which lenders distance themselves from ever being accused of having any influence over a valuation firm and valuer. However, most firms on the panel are professional and have integrity and, therefore, there is an argument that even if a lender can choose a valuation firm, the firm will remain objective. Lenders have a list of valuers they will accept for the valuation of a property they are considering lending against. This is known as a panel.

Adversely, there are a couple of valuation firms on the panel — that continue to remain on the panel — who are engaged to value certain types of properties that they have explicitly stated, in public, they dislike. So it begs the question: why should they be allowed to be used for valuing these types of properties, or conduct valuations in areas, when they have mentioned (to the market) that they just don't like them? There is a possible conflict of interest.

It can be difficult for a lender or individual to get a valuation reassigned to another lender, but it is possible. There may be a charge for another valuation to be conducted, even if it's with the same valuation firm — and even the same valuer!

One reason that valuations are not reassigned is that each lender has certain criteria they wish the valuer to address in the report. So, one lender's criteria may be different from another, and what one lender wants can be meaningless to another lender.

Loan-to-Value Ratio (LVR)

This refers to the loan-to-value ratio, which means that if a property is priced at $400,000 then most lenders will go up to 90% debt against the value; some lenders will go as high as 95%.

The lenders mortgage insurance providers recently ceased allowing the LMI premium to be added to the loan for investment property purchases above 95%.

Owner Builder Loans

Some people still think they can, and should be able to, get a loan for building their own dwelling on their land. Sometimes the individual is a qualified builder, and some inexperienced brokers consider this makes it more acceptable. The reality is that whether the individual is a builder or not, emotion is involved when it's your own house. Cost overruns are common, due to changes, upgrades, and so on. This is why lenders, on the whole, tend to avoid owner builder loans. One or two lenders still do it, although at reduced loan-to-value ratios.

Credit Reporting Association of Australia (CRAA)

One reason why a deal may have to go to a different lender is due to poor repayment history — that is, the client not living up to their responsibilities in repaying the loan on time. Defaults on the CRAA are another problem. Many applicants/consumers do not consider a paid default relating to three years earlier to be much of a problem, and may, often, not inform their broker that they have a default history.

Defaults and judgements can remain on the CRAA for typically five years, and will not be removed unless paid. Some people offer to pay this to get the new loan they are after; in many instances they are obliged to pay it anyway, so they are not doing themselves any favours by offering to pay it now. It should have been paid anyway. It can be noticed, on the CRAA, if the applicant was aware of it as well. Maybe they applied for credit a few months earlier, in which case they would have been informed of the situation by the lender at that time — especially if their request for that loan was denied.

A person's CRAA report — once known as a VEDA report — records all activity when applying for a loan, or debt, or even enquiring about debt (maybe via a credit card, store card at a shopping centre, personal loan, car loan, business loan, and mortgage) with a lender. It is sometimes evident that people have been shopping around to

135

different lenders, and if there are too many enquiries on the CRAA, lenders will not like it.

Most lenders have a credit scoring system, and both loan mortgage insurers do as well. This gives a person a score on the CRAA: the lower the score the more unfavourable the CRAA is for lending purposes. This is another reason why it is important to choose the best broker — they will know who does 'credit score'. Sometimes it may be necessary to avoid lenders that 'credit score', and sometimes it's only possible to borrow 80% loan-to-value ratio as the deal may fail on the credit scoring software of LMI providers.

The Five Cs of Lending

1. Commitment
2. Collateral (Property — what the valuation says, zoning, density, postcode)
3. Character
4. Conditions (Policy)
5. Capacity (Servicing)

Commitment

Lenders want to see a track record of repayments on debts before they are willing to trust someone enough to be responsible. Often I see someone fail credit scoring because they don't have any debt, and no history of paying repayments on debt. It's therefore indeterminable whether that person has the inclination to repay the debt. Deals, where someone has 5% of genuine savings are good, because they have proven they can save money. Often first home buyers may not have saved their 5%, and they are granted a hand-out from family. Then, by the time they receive the first homebuyers grant and the loan mortgage insurance is capitalised, they have put in close to nothing. There is no 'hurt money' in the deal and no 'skin in the game' as it were. It is understandable why lenders fail these people on credit scoring. These type of clients end up with a specialist lender (or a 'non-conforming lender') who charges more but can offer the person the loan they want.

Collateral

Having assets is another strength in a deal when applying for a mortgage. Whether it's your cars, furniture, and other belongings that you have given a value to, or property, shares, superannuation, and cash, they all count to paint a picture. The older you get in age, the more assets the lenders would like to see. They don't like it when they see a sixty-year-old person renting with friends, with no assets. They tend to consider the applicant as a significant lending risk whilst divorce can often explain this unpleasantly poor situation the individual is in, it may not explain it all of the time. Lenders don't see things as 'glass half-full'. They often put the burden of proof on the shoulders of the applicant, to counter the immediate seeds of doubt that have grown in the minds of the credit assessors.

Character

Character is particularly studied in someone who has not paid their bills or repayments on time. They have defaults, tax debt, bankruptcy, judgements, and so on. This is often the type of individual the lenders frown upon. These people end up on higher rates with specialist lenders. Some people are dishonest and do not disclose all of their liabilities (i.e. credit cards) on the application form and lenders are unforgiving when this happens — and rightly so.

Sometimes, defaults do end up on someone's credit file without them knowing, due to oversights, or simply forgetting about something. Thousands of other excuses simply 'don't cut the mustard'. A common excuse is that the individual 'went away and left a friend to take responsibility for paying the debt'. A default won't be recorded in as little as a week or three though. The wrong would have occurred over, say, a three-month period.

Some people are debt junkies. They apply for short-term loans, or they apply for various credit cards and personal loans, or simply tyre-kick their way around the mortgage industry looking for the best rate. Lenders look upon these people unfavourably, and if these people have too many enquiries on their CRAA (credit report) they have a greater likelihood of failing credit scoring.

Most of the time credit hits are incurred because the individual is unaware that every time they apply for a mobile phone contract, change energy providers, and/or purchase a lounge suite or television on credit from a store, they end up with a credit hit. These types of 'hits' are generally acceptable, but when a lender sees three attempts to get a mortgage approved, at three different lenders, they will usually fail that applicant — and the applicant ends up with a specialist lender.

Sometimes it is a broker who has not done their homework and placed the loan with a lender before confirming if that lender will do the application. Often I see deals where the broker has simply not done a servicing calculator before submitting the loan. Some brokers even send mass 'bcc addressed' emails around the industry looking for an answer because they've not done their homework.

Conditions

Policy governs how a deal is assessed. This is the more tangible method of assessing a loan and its credit worthiness. This is less about the borrower and more about the purpose of the loan, type of loan, loan amount, etc. There are parameters for lending based on location, debt against equity, loan amount, and purpose.

Capacity

What a person earns in the role they perform in their job, and how long they have been working in that role, both have an impact on the loan deal being approved. A person must be able to service the debt they require, in conjunction with any other debts they already have.

This is another reason why a broker is better than a bank. A good broker is one who knows which calculators are better, and which lenders are more forgiving. With a pay as you earn (PAYE) person (an employee) their base wage is the main factor for servicing the loan. Should they also receive commissions and bonuses these generally need to be evidenced over two years and averaged; with some lenders, they will only require six months of evidence for commissions. Overtime, shift work, and fringe benefits, are looked at differently with various lenders, with some needing a letter from the employer stating it is ongoing, and will be consistent. Other lenders need twelve months of evidence in conjunction with this letter. Probation is normally not possible over 80% LVR. One-day employment can be possible, as long as there is evidence of twelve months in the same role and industry experience.

When working for family or a partner, wage slips have a risk of being doctored, and fictitious. Likewise, the wife of the owner often doesn't receive regular and consistent monies into an account, even though she can provide payslips to suggest she does. Many lenders ask for three months of bank statements to support the receipt of said income. Blood can be thicker than water they say.

With regard to salary sacrifice, some lenders do not input the income as un-taxed; because it is income the person is not receiving directly, and therefore cannot be used for servicing anyway. Some lenders will add back to the gross wage a percentage of the fringe benefit tax (FBT) on the group certificate.

Many lenders sensitise the rate, so if the repayment rate is let's say 5% variable, they may add up to 2% to the rate. One lender actually uses a standard qualifying rate of 8%, even though their rates are down below 5.5%. This loading on rate is often on all debt, so it's not just what you are applying for but also on existing debts as well. I recommend considering to use a lender who services existing debt on existing rate/repayments (including servicing existing repayments as they are.) This means if they are 'interest only loans' then they use interest only repayments; likewise for principle and interest loans. This type of calculator is quite advantageous to investors. Make sure the lender includes deductable debt on the calculator.

If you own a property with a friend, and you have agreed to share the repayments *or* you have possibly agreed to have two separate splits (loans against the one property) so that you can each pay your respective payments. Do not forget that most lenders still deem you to be jointly and severally liable for your debt *and* your friend's debt. Lenders do not care about any private arrangement you may have in place. Likewise, if you only receive half the rent due to being 50% on title, the lender will normally only use half the rental income total towards servicing another debt. This occurs even though they will allocate the entire liability to your name, based on the debt you have with your friend. Some lenders do, however, look at things in a way that you may find fairer, in that they attribute half the debt and half the rent.

Exit Strategies

Exit Strategies are important, and lenders often require one when a borrower is between, or beyond, the ages of 55-60 years, and they need to show an ability to repay the loan when they cease work. Their type of work industry has a bearing too. For example, if the borrower is employed in a labour intensive role they are more unlikely to work for another ten years, in comparison to someone in an office or administrative role. There is less wear and tear on the body; therefore, an office or administrative person would potentially work for a few more years.

Nonetheless, these people normally must have equity in investment properties, or value in shares and superannuation, to be able to use in paying off the loan. Simply downsizing is a throwaway line that applicants use far too often, to try and demonstrate an exit strategy. They may also nominate that they are selling their business. Lenders do not want to subscribe to be complicit, or implicated, in someone being forced to sell their house or business. People change their minds as they get older, and could easily twist the situation around. They could then, suddenly, end up as a sob story on A Current Affair, where someone is being sold-up by a bank.

Not that I wish to judge the unfortunate situations people find themselves in, in life, but there are cases where a person has said they would downsize, then they get sick and cannot work anymore, then the bank is called to task for wanting their repayments made. It is best for lenders to avoid these situations under responsible lending. This is, at least, the opinion of many credit assessors.

Loan Mortgage Insurance (LMI)

Most lenders, offering normal-priced rates, will mortgage insure their loans above 80% LVR if it is a full documentation loan, and over 60% LVR if it is a limited, or low documentation loan (i.e. self-employed people who have not completed their tax returns.)

LMI may be able to be added on top of the loan. If you wish to avoid LMI you will have to use more of your cash or equity. Borrowing more for investment properties gives you more tax deductable interest, it uses less of your own money by the higher gearing/leverage, and it could help you purchase more properties (depending on the overall cost of debt.)

You should consider having a balanced approach for weighing up whether you have a bigger loan. which in turn will have more of a negative impact on servicing with the greater cost of debt) This also puts you in a position of starting out with less equity in the purchased property (therefore exposing you to more risk if the market has a downturn), Compare this to using more of your cash or equity reserves, which can also lead to less money or equity available for future property purchases

LMI will be cheaper if the LVR (or debt) is lower. If you are using two properties, one as a refinance and one as a purchase, besides all the other benefits of not cross securing your assets with the one lender; this may also give you the benefit of paying less LMI to achieve the same outcome.

How to get the bank to say yes more than once

If you wish to continue to purchase investment property it is important to use different lenders to suit your purpose and the type of loan you require. You also need to consider the type of property you are purchasing, the strength of your income in servicing the loan, and your existing exposure to the lender.

It becomes more of a risk to the borrower if they expose themselves to a bank for more than one property. Three or four properties would be the limit, typically, if an investor was to continue going back to the same lender: lenders then become increasingly reluctant to continue exposing themselves to the borrower; it also becomes very risky for the borrower, as the bank has access to several properties and could force the sale of all of them.

The 'all monies clause' (the ability for a lender to recall all loans, and force you to sell or refinance) is not something that I would consider a frequent problem. Many property spruikers still go around promoting the 'all monies clause' as a big problem. This is designed as a scare tactic to lead people to believe that the spruiker's finance department can do a better job than an independent broker. Many property spruiking firms have their own finance divisions (professing to being the best at helping you arrange finance, often at higher rates than through a normal broker) and they wield this 'all monies clause' around for their own gain. This ploy has been widely used, since the year 2000, in convincing investors to go with other second-tier lenders who used to pay the broker more commissions.

Low Doc Loans

This refers to loans in a time when less documentation was required. When low doc loans were established, they were meant to help people who had legitimately not had time to complete their tax returns. Unfortunately, this has been abused to the point of it having become a joke prior to the GFC in Australia. I won't touch on America, because it is too farcical to waste time on how loose and unregulated their market was. Corruption went all the way to the top.

Banks used to give PAYG (employed people) a low doc loans based on certain criteria, such as not being able to prove alleged commissions and bonuses, etc. Post GFC, this type of low doc loan has been removed from lender offerings, as has what was called a 'no doc loan', where nothing needed to be provided regarding income, and someone could get a loan. Some brokers, I might add, are still incompetent enough to be asking for this type of loan for their clients, right up to August 2013.

Brokers

There are many benefits attached to using a broker, the industry they operate in is known as 'third party' because brokers have access to a panel of lenders, and brokers offer you the lenders' products. Therefore, the products are not being offered directly to you (the consumer) from the lender. They are offered through a third party (i.e. the broker.)

A mortgage broker is vital, and I recommend using a broker for many reasons, one that stands out for a growing property investor is that the broker can compare the different servicing calculators of different lenders to try to make the deal work.

Servicing is the main element of many that the lender focuses on when deciding if they want to continue saying yes to the applicant. The borrowing capacity varies between lenders, as does lending policy and the types of income that are acceptable (as well as the percentage of those incomes.)

Brokers can compare many choices — a service that one bank cannot offer you and others probably can and a good broker will find it. Be aware, though, that some brokers will only use the 'big four' banks, and one or two 'other' banks. This is lazy and is evidence (in my mind) of poor business and sales skills. One reason is that a broker should really be there to offer choices to their clients, which may not always be available at a bank branch.

A true broker, in my opinion, compares loans and then offers their client unbiased and independent choices, which include the products from non-banks as well as banks. They are not purely rate driven, but rather, focus on policy, turnaround times (time it takes from submitting your loan to settlement) and choosing a lender which can provide timely communication. The best rate is not the best loan.

Many brokers are incentivised by the banks through being given a preferential status — which includes higher commissions and better treatment than other brokers receive.

I have dealt with banks directly for some of my loans and I have used a broker for other loans. If you're looking into your first investment property or your 20th, I think you need a broker; the type of property can limit the choice of lender as well. Luckily I understood what I wanted, and where I wanted it which is why I initially used a bank. I clearly understood my financial situation; unless you are sure about what you a doing, then use a broker. After investing in the first few properties, though, it became important to find the best servicing calculator (the calculator that provided the largest loan based on my situation, and on the property to be purchased) and to free up my time.

Some of the reasons that I think using a broker can be highly beneficial (besides saving time in finding a lender suitable for your needs) are that they chase documents for you, and you may get a better deal due to their relationships with some of the lenders (better than if you went direct sometimes.) A good broker is there to help you understand the loan documents, and they shop around before submitting your loan.

Most brokers are excellent and I can help you find the better ones.

Many brokers use the big four Australian banks (NAB, Westpac, ANZ and CBA) more often than other lenders. Often it may not be the broker's fault that they end up using banks the majority of the time. The groups they belong to (known as aggregators) often charge huge sponsorship fees to lenders in order to be provided the ability to have a presence at one of the aggregators' knowledge/product development days. Some smaller lenders cannot afford these fees and unfortunately are not authorised to attend, meaning the brokers are in many ways limited to using the banks that pay the largest sponsorship and forced into having limited access to other lenders that often do a better job for their clients.

This is wrong. Brokers should have contact and access to knowledge from more than just the lenders with the deepest pockets in order to gain better knowledge of all the products at their disposal. We are talking tens and tens of thousands of dollars just to have a lender representative be allowed to make an appearance at a Christmas party or a knowledge development day.

At one stage, I phoned a broker aggregator enquiring about their Christmas function and was informed that even though the lender I worked for had provided excellent service to this group's brokers, and maintained regular contact with the brokers, we were not invited to mingle with the brokers at the party as we had not succumbed to the extortionate sponsorship fees required by this aggregator. Amounts of $50k-150k pa plus have been thrown around, and in return you get a table or stand two to three times a year at a knowledge sharing day, and sometimes just a free sausage and beer at their Christmas party.

Applicants themselves do silly things, such as shop around for the best rate, making enquiries, signing a privacy statement and, inadvertently, degrading the quality of their own credit history. Each time a person shops around, a credit hit on their credit history may be generated, making it less palatable for a lender to want to deal with that borrower. Let the broker do all this for you.

Best ways to structure your loans so you can continue borrowing

Some lenders service existing debt at existing rates and that means the servicing calculator can work in an investor's favour, if they have other property debts.

Some calculators do not take into account deductable interest, which leads to a negative impact on servicing. Speak to a good broker who actually compares products from non-banks as well as other banks, as already suggested. A borrowing capacity can differ by many hundreds of thousands of dollars. Personally, I recently compared two lenders, a bank and a non-bank. The non-bank would allow me to borrow $600,000 more than the bank.

Self-employed borrowers do sometimes prefer to avoid tax rather than to increase their taxable income on paper, which, in turn, could aid in increasing their borrowing capacity. This leads them to try and get a 'low documentation' or 'alternative documentation loan' and, whilst these loans serve a purpose, they can be more expensive, which in turn reduces one's borrowing capacity moving forward — **and** it increases the repayments on the loan. So, if a borrower is more willing to provide their tax returns, and those tax returns show enough income, they could then be eligible for a better rate, making it easier to potentially borrow more for the next investment purchase.

Avoid cross-collateralising your loans, and don't expose yourself to the one lender more than you really need to.

Should you avoid LMI or use it? If using LMI, how do you do it safely? Using or avoiding LMI can be determined by the amount of equity a person has available.

Consider avoiding LMI. This can assist in avoiding credit scoring. Credit scoring is an automated way that some lenders (and certainly the mortgage insurers) commence an assessment on you as a borrower and — if you have too much exposure to low doc loans or LMI insured loans — your score can end up being lower, which could inhibit your being able to borrow more money. A number of non-banks do not credit score though, even up to 95%.

Using LMI increases the loan-to-value ratio on the investment property, and reduces the amount of equity from another property that would otherwise be required to complete the purchase.

The cost of stamp duty may have a bearing on the need to use LMI, as a person's cash or equity may only be enough to complete the purchase, but may not be enough for stamp duty as well. This could possibly lead to needing to borrow more against the investment property. Therefore, LMI providers can be necessary and useful.

Postcodes can be a determining factor in whether a lender wants to lend in a particular area. Some lenders have internal sign-off with LMI policy so this can be overcome. Some lenders can avoid LMI.

LMI providers do 'credit score', which can put the loan at risk of not being approved. Banks also, typically, credit score. So, again, be careful which mortgage broker you are using, as a lazy or poor broker can lead to your loan being declined, due to that broker submitting your loan to the wrong lender, or by not using a more appropriate one. And so I reinforce my opinion that **you should** use a mortgage broker.

LMI serve a purpose but at a cost. The cost can vary in range, and can end up being in the tens of thousands of dollars and, if you have not done your research, this can unnecessarily eat into your capital/ capital gain. Also bear in mind that it can eat into your cash flow, as you not only pay this insurance, but you also end up paying interest on this insurance amount if you borrow it on top of the loan, or within the loan.

An LMI approved deal can allow you to borrow up to 95% against an investment property but, with recent changes, the LMI can no longer be added (capitalized) to the loan above 95% on an investment property. Non-LMI loans to 95% are also available.

If you are looking at ways of dealing with LMI insurers safely, per se, then please ensure you deal with the right broker — one who either has excellent knowledge of LMI policy, or one who has easy and good communication with the relationship manager of a lender. In my experience, non-bank relationship managers provide an excellent service to brokers, and their rates and policy can often be better and more flexible.

What are the steps you need to take so you don't have to refinance each time you want to buy a property?

Set up a redraw facility, so you have the equity available and ready for the next opportunity. Lenders are not really your friend — they are a business out to make money, and the less you have to deal with them for each purchase, the easier you can invest, and the quicker you can act on an opportunity. You would then be more in control of what you want to do.

Requirements for an application to be submitted

It can be different for each lender. The list, below, will suit most lenders:

- Two forms of ID — one of them being a photo ID (such as driver's licence, or passport), and one additional form of ID such as rates notice, birth certificate, tax return and assessment notice, or Medicare card.
- Two forms of income evidence for an employee — starting with payslips (two), letter from an employer, and/or group certificate.
- Repayment statements for six months — if it is a refinance situation.
- Three months of credit card, personal loan, and/or car loan statements.
- Council rates notice.

- The broker will have to provide a servicing calculator and notes summarising your situation.
- If you are making a purchase you will need the purchase contract. If it's for a 'house and land' then you'll need to supply the land and fixed price construction contract.
- Rental statements for any investment properties.
- Remember: include all credit card limits and amounts owing, not forgetting HECS debts, and store cards.

Assets versus non-assets

The fundamental idea of Robert Kiyosaki is that there are good assets and there are bad assets. Bad assets are liabilities.

> *'The poor and the middle class work for money.*
> *The rich have money work for them.'*
> **— Robert Kiyosaki**

Traditionally, a liability is a cost. It is money outflow. However, a liability is anything that does not produce income.

Some common liabilities are listed below:

Motorbike — some people purchase these to work on them, ride them, simply look at them, or maybe it's part of a temporary emotional weakness (such as mid-life crisis.) Someone having a mid-life crisis possibly feels trapped in their life, or reflects on what little they have achieved in life, or they begin to face the reality that eludes most people in younger years: what will they retire on? What will they live off? Is there an easier way? Then it becomes an exercise in masochism by wasting $20,000 on a motorbike, rather than investing in something that will make money.

Boat and caravan — parked in the yard and used once a week (if they're lucky), or possibly a few times a year.

Mortgage on your home — taken out, but not for the purpose of investing in property. Your rates, water/gas/electricity, etc., are all liabilities. These costs are unavoidable in your own home but, at least, with an investment property, the associated costs are simply the cost of doing business, as it were.

Cars — many people like to drive a nice car. It makes them feel good, it is an ego boost, and they can show off. Many people with expensive cars have high-cost leases on them. The money going into this lease could be used to afford an investment property. I learned (early on) never to buy a new car. You lose 40% value the moment you take ownership. A car will not make money normally — unless it is extremely rare. Buy a car that is reliable and presentable, but not a 'showpiece' either.

My interview with a mortgage broker Michael Sugiandi

http://www.austpag.com.au/premium-content

Chapter 9

Accounting "The Money"

Tax laws are complicated and always changing. An accountant may address a particular issue, and then find this opens a whole 'can of worms'. For instance you can structure the ownership to take advantage of the 'now', but where does this position put you the taxpayer for capital gains tax in the future? There are many 'grey areas', where the law is not clear and is open to incorrect interpretation and it takes knowledge and experience to make the best decision.

When entering into the property investment arena, it is essential to set the correct foundations. This includes selecting good property that will appreciate in value, financing it correctly, ensuring the ownership is as advantageous as possible, and then taking advantage of every means available to make the property affordable to hold.

Affordability

An accountant's role is to help you look after your money: they want to minimise the holding costs of the investment and ensure the property is as affordable as possible.

Firstly, it is vital that the right property is purchased, and that there is not a likelihood of extended vacancies.

A client's financial situation should be assessed before purchasing a property. An accountant or property advisor can give an estimate of the weekly out-of-pocket cost you can expect to incur. Clients are often amazed at how affordable holding a property can be for their particular situation. On the other hand it may be out of their reach at present, and they have to save or earn a little more.

It is important for you to not suffer with interest rate rises. Scenarios of one or two percent interest rate increases can be factored in to demonstrate what the extra cost is likely to be, helping to ensure you are able to accommodate this sort of rise.

When the investor has set their sights on a particular property, and has received some detailed information, a good accountant and property advisor can provide a cash flow that will demonstrate the real out of pocket expenses and after-tax cost per week — not what spruikers and developers are telling you.

A combination of correct ownership structure, financing, depreciation reports, and tax instalment deduction variations all work together to ensure that the cost of holding the property is minimised.

Some of the key areas that you can ask your accountant to address are:

- Structuring
- Financing
- Tax Depreciation Report — existing property versus new property
- Tax instalment deduction variation

Structuring

Establishing the correct foundation through structuring is vital and it is very important to receive sound advice from an expert in this field — not a mate, or the bloke at the pub, or the real estate agent.

Generally, the capital gains, losses on sale, and profits and losses incurred each year, must be apportioned according to the ownership on the title, not who is on the loan.

There is no one ideal structure for holding investment property, but it is important to take into account the personal goals, work goals, and how long the property is likely to be held for. If a couple is purchasing the property, is one party likely to cease work in the short term, or return to work? What are the projected incomes?

Does the client wish to build a portfolio of property? Are the properties likely to become positively geared within the next few years, or is the investor in the position to positively gear some property?

What about asset protection? Maybe one of the parties owns a business and it is important not to have valuable assets in their name.

Ownership as an individual or partnership

If a couple purchases a property, under joint ownership, the ownership defaults to 50:50 ownership.

However, should two or more people be purchasing a property and wish to vary the ownership to suit their situation, then the property needs to be purchased under 'tenants in common'. This not only allows flexibility in ownership percentages, but also allows each party to will their share of the property to a beneficiary of their choice, which is not the case with joint ownership.

If it is expected that the property will be negatively geared for a number of years and the negative gearing benefits are likely to be substantial, then it makes sense for the higher income earner to own more of the asset and offset the tax deduction against the higher income.

A disadvantage of this strategy is that if the asset becomes positively geared or is sold and a capital gain is made, that net profit or capital gain will be taxed at the individual's high marginal tax rate.

Company or Trust

A significant disadvantage of holding a negatively geared property in a company or trust is that excess losses are 'trapped' in the company or trust. They cannot be used to offset the investor's taxable income with the intention to deliver an attractive refund to assist with the costs of holding the property.

The losses are carried forward in the trust and can be used to offset future profits generated in the company or trust. However these losses do not offset future capital gains, much to the disappointment of many investors. Capital gains can only be offset by capital losses.

Accountants generally advise against the use of a company to hold an investment property. A company could be used to hold a property if it is positively geared and the investor wishes to use the 30% company tax rate, or help with asset protection.

However a company does not give the asset protection that a discretionary trust does, as the shares owned by a taxpayer are assets and can be sold to satisfy the debts of a taxpayer.

The most significant disadvantage of holding property in a company is that it is not entitled to a 50% discount on capital gains, which an individual taxpayer is entitled to. Not being able to access the CGT discount is a disincentive for holding assets in companies.

A discretionary trust however provides superior asset protection because even if an individual taxpayer is bankrupted the assets in the trust are protected as the individual owns no interest in a discretionary trust.

A discretionary trust can be used to distribute capital gains to beneficiaries in an effective manner, and the individual beneficiary is also able to obtain a 50% discount on capital gains tax in their own individual returns.

Tax Depreciation Report

Investors who purchased a property that was built after 16 September 1987 are entitled to claim a 2.5% depreciation rate on the cost of the building. It is this claim for cost of construction that can make a property much more affordable for the investor, as a significant deduction can be claimed without the requirement to make a cash outlay.

It is important to be aware of a not very publicised fact, that this 2.5% building write off reduces the cost base of the property and will increase capital gains tax when you sell it. However, it is twice as effective to claim the 2.5% deduction due to the 50% capital gains tax discount.

It can work well for an investor who is on a high income to provide a good tax deduction, but doesn't plan to sell the property until they retire or their income is reduced.

As previously mentioned, this report is best obtained through a quantity surveyor for a cost of approximately $600 to $700. This cost is well and truly covered in the first year through tax savings, and the cost of the report is also tax deductible.

Tax Instalment Deduction Form (TID)

Instead of waiting for the nice big refund when your tax return is lodged at the end of the financial year, the tax office allows the investor to submit a 'tax variation form', which authorises an employer to deduct a reduced amount of tax from the employee's regular pay. This gives the investor extra money in their pocket throughout the year; do remember that the year-end refund will be reduced.

So, instead of waiting for a refund cheque of, say, $5000 after 30 June, the investor can receive an extra $100 per week in their pay packet throughout the entire year. The Australian Tax Office (ATO) doesn't pay you interest because you waited for your refund, so it's far better that you, the taxpayer, have the money working to save interest throughout the year.

It is important to stress that care does need to be taken when lodging a TID variation. It is a provisional tax return based on estimates for the upcoming financial year. It is important to err on the side of being conservative when calculating expenses, rather than finding you have not paid enough tax throughout the year.

What Expenses Can You Claim?

Typically there are four categories accountants work with.

1. Is the expense not deductible because it is private in nature? (e.g. holiday house)
2. Can an immediate deduction be claimed in this year?
3. Does the expense need to be claimed over a number of years? (i.e. depreciation of fixtures & fittings)
4. Does the expense need to form part of the capital cost?

a.   If so, is it part of the building and therefore can be written off at 2.5% pa?

b.   Is it not part of the building (e.g. landscaping) and can only be included in the capital cost written off over a different time frame?

Not Deductible

If an investment property is not earning rental income, then expenses cannot be deducted. For instance, expenses on a vacant block of land need to be capitalised and included in the cost base for the capital gains tax calculation, unless the property is earning, for example, agistment income.

If a holiday home is let for part of the year then expenses must be apportioned between the rental period and private use.

Immediate Deductions

To claim these expenses the property must be available for rent. You would need to show that the property is listed for rental with an agent, or that you have been advertising it, and that the requested rent is consistent with the market. This list is not exhaustive but outlines the typical deductions that can be claimed in the annual rental property return.

Further information for items marked with an asterisk (*) is provided below this list.

- Council and water rates
- Insurance, such as building and contents, and public liability
- Land tax

- Repairs and maintenance *
- Gardening and lawn mowing
- Interest on loans *
- Agents fees and commissions
- Body corporate fees *
- Advertising for tenants *
- Travel to collect rent, inspect or maintain the property *
- Stationery, telephone and postage
- Legal expenses (incurred in relation to tenant, not acquisition or disposal)
- Borrowing expenses

Repairs and maintenance

The deductibility of repairs and maintenance can be a very grey area. For instance, painting would normally be considered maintenance, and be fully deductible in the year the expense is incurred. However, if the home was newly acquired and needed to the painted at that time, the painting is considered to be part of 'initial repairs' and forms part of the capital cost. Judgment needs to be exercised to ascertain at which point the painting is no longer classified as 'initial repairs'.

Repairs generally relate directly to wear and tear or other damage that occurred as a result of renting out the property. For example, if tenants have damaged the property in the early years, then painting becomes a repair. Should this occur, it is recommended you take photos as evidence of any damage caused by tenants.

However if you are planning to rent out your main residence, or even a property you have inherited, and painting needs to be undertaken to get the property ready for rental then the painting *can* be claimed in the first year.

Interest on loans

Should a loan be taken out to purchase a rental property, the interest charged on that loan can be claimed as a deduction. However, the property must be rented, or available for rental, in the income year for which you claim a deduction. If not, then the income is not deductible or must be apportioned.

If you choose a line of credit to finance your property purchase, it is recommended that the loan not be used for private purposes. If there is a fluctuating balance due to a variety of deposits and withdrawals, and it is used for both private purposes and rental property purposes, it can quickly diminish the amount of interest that can be claimed as a tax deduction. The calculation of interest than can be included in the rental deductions is also quite involved and time-consuming.

Travel to collect rent, inspect or maintain the property

There is a fallacy out there that you are allowed two trips to inspect a property per year. This has possibly arisen in the belief that this is reasonable as far as the tax department is concerned. However, claiming two trips per annum to travel interstate to 'inspect rental properties' is likely to be considered very unusual.

On the other hand, if you have decided to personally collect the rent, or undertake the garden maintenance for your property, then monthly visits (i.e. twelve trips per annum) would not be unreasonable.

With interstate property, if you fly to inspect the property, stay overnight, and return home the following day, the airfare and accommodation expenses would be allowed provided the whole purpose of the trip was to inspect the rental property.

However, should the trip be combined with a holiday, then the expenses may need to be apportioned, taking into account the main purpose of the trip. Was the holiday incidental to the trip, or was the inspection of the property incidental to the trip?

Body corporate fees covering general maintenance and administration are deductible in the year incurred, though if funds are put aside for a special purpose fund and used for capital expenditure, then this expense must be capitalised.

Expenses Deductible Over a Number of Income Years

There are three types of expenses you may incur for your rental property that may be claimed over a number of income years:

- Borrowing expenses
- Amounts for decline in value of depreciating assets
- Capital works deductions.

Borrowing expenses

These are expenses directly incurred in taking out a loan. If total expenses are less than $100 the expense can be written off in the same year, otherwise the expenses are claimed over a period of five years or the period of the loan.

Decline in value of depreciating assets

Depreciating assets are generally items than can be easily removed and replaced and not part of the building structure. For example, a free-standing bookcase can be depreciated at the higher depreciation rates, but a built-in bookshelf must be claimed at just 2.5% as part of the cost of construction or special building write-off.

The types of fixtures and fittings (plant and equipment) that the tax office allows you to claim deductions for are items such as stoves, dishwashers, curtains, heaters, air conditioners, and carpet. The depreciation rates typically range from 10% to 25% of the cost per item; this can be claimed per annum. If items are less than $1000 in value they can be added to a 'low value pool' and written off at 18.75% in the first year and 37.5% thereon.

Plant and equipment costing less than $300 per owner can be written off each year. For example, for joint owners items under $600 can be written off as the cost of the item is split between the owners, resulting in $300 each.

Capital Costs

I referred earlier to gaining a building surveyor's report and it is in this that the capital cost of constructing the building can be written off at 2.5% for normal residential property over the next forty years. This applies to property built after 16 September 1987 and is often referred to as 'special building write-off'.

It is calculated on the original cost of constructing the building, plus improvements at their original cost. It has nothing to do with the purchase price of the home.

Up until May 1997 this building write-off was of significant benefit as the capital cost claimed did not have to reduce the cost base of the building, and therefore the capital gain wasn't increased. However the building write-off applied to properties built since this date reduces the original cost of the property and therefore increases the capital gain.

Capital Gains Tax

If you acquired a property after 19 September 1985 you may make a capital gain or capital loss when you sell the property or your share in the property.

You will make a capital gain from the sale of your rental property to the extent that the capital proceeds received are more than the cost base of the property. You will make a capital loss to the extent that the property's reduced cost base exceeds those capital proceeds. If you are a co-owner of an investment property, you will make a capital gain or loss according to your ownership interest in the property.

The cost base and reduced cost base of a property includes the amount you paid for it together with certain incidental costs associated with acquiring, holding, and disposing of it (for example, legal fees, stamp duty, and real estate agent's commissions.) Certain amounts that you have deducted or which you can deduct are excluded from the property's cost base or reduced cost base.

You may then quality for a 50% discount on the capital gain, provided you hold the property for more than twelve months.

Your capital gain or capital loss may be disregarded if a rollover applies (e.g. if your property was destroyed or compulsorily acquired, or you transferred it to your former spouse under a court order following the breakdown of your marriage.)

Often investors become very worried about capital gains tax; keep in mind that because of the 50% discount you will generally not pay more than 15% tax on your gain. This means that you keep up to 85% of the gain.

What Do You Give Your Accountant at Tax Time?

Your investment property should be a passive investment (investment taking very little of your time) that should make money for you without being a burden. If you get your real estate agent to pay for everything, it will minimise your workload. If you have to pay for something yourself, please keep a record and take it to your accountant at tax time. The accountant does not need the receipt, but it is important that you hold the receipt.

In the first year of purchase you need to bring the following with you:

a.   Quantity surveyor's depreciation report (if relevant)
b.   The conveyancing settlement letter and notice of adjustments
c.   Real estate rental property summary
d.   Bank statements for the loan
e.   Summarise extra payments made that were excluded from the statement from the real estate agent. It is important to never throw receipts away, even after five years, as they are essential in the case of an ATO audit, and to assist with calculating capital gain in the future.

In your second year, and all subsequent years, you must bring everything included in the above list, except for items (a) and (b).

Case Study

'I have been in public practice for over twenty years now, and have worked with hundreds of property investors. I have seen the successes and the failures. I have seen the investors who have failed to consult with their accountant or expert adviser, and have made bad and costly decisions. This may have been due to poor choice of property, poor

structuring of ownership, and/or not ensuring the affordability of the property has been maximised.

'Just a few things that I have seen investors do are:

- *Buy several negatively geared properties at once and find that there are no tax advantages in holding two of the properties because the tax losses not only placed their income below the tax-free threshold, but actually resulted in a negative income outcome.*
- *Buy properties in a trust and expect the losses to be transferred to the individual return and deliver a lovely refund.*
- *On the advice of a 'friend' buy two properties in a company structure, which now means there are no capital gains tax concessions should the properties be sold.*
- *Been caught by property spruikers and developers and purchased properties that have lost value and/or haven't been tenanted as expected. Because the clients couldn't afford to hold the properties without tenants, they have been sold at a loss, and the sale price hasn't even covered the borrowings.*
- *Clients who have purchased an old property, poured significant funds into renovating, and then discover these renovations are not tax deductible in their first tax return and must be included in the capital cost of acquiring the property. (Investors may gain some consolation from the fact that it may be possible for these improvements to be depreciated at 2.5% per annum.)*
- *Property in joint names where half of all the losses are wasted because one is not earning income and is not likely to.*
- *Properties purchased and tax returns prepared over a number of years where the buyer had no knowledge that they could be claiming extra deductions of $3000 to $4000 per annum that don't require a cash outlay.'*

— **Coral Page, Accountant**

It is always wise to seek advice.

Follow this link to view my interview with Coral Page

http://www.austpag.com.au/premium-content

Property within an SMSF

In recent years there has been considerable publicity regarding purchasing residential property in a self-managed superfund.

This structure is only for some. It does have the advantages of the ultimate asset protection, and tax relief. However, for these tax benefits to be relevant, the property is locked away until the beneficiaries are of an acceptable age.

It is generally considered important that the fund retains liquidity (i.e. holds assets such as cash and securities that can be quickly converted to cash), so a good balance of liquid assets as well as a property may be wise.

A good accountant may have the view that if residential property is to be held in a self-managed superfund the deposit should be large enough to ensure that the property is positively geared, particularly when the limits for contributing to the superfund are capped at such a low level.

Rules governing SMSFs are always changing. The advantages of having an SMSF are dependent on many things. This part of the book is not suggesting what you should do or not do; it is merely to inform you how things work with an SMSF.

Since the mid 1980s people have wanted greater autonomy in managing their superannuation fund. As of the mid '80s people were able to set-up and manage their own self-managed super fund, allowing them to make their own investment decisions and in turn hopefully providing the necessary returns for each member as they approach retirement. Tax concession benefits provide income for retirement to each member's benefit, as they do in a normal superannuation fund, so it is not the reason why someone would set up a SMSF.

SMSFs have become very popular over recent years for a number of reasons. Most recently it is the ability to purchase property in the fund. John Howard abolished the ban in 2007 preventing people from borrowing money in their SMSF to invest. Members of their own SMSF can acquire and hold real estate whether residential or commercial business property.

Other reasons that have been around a lot longer may be the possible, but not to be relied on, potential of it being more cost effective to have your own fund rather than a non SMSF — some larger superannuation funds charge very high fees. The Superannuation Industry Supervision (SIS) Act's requirements may be more beneficial to some people when compared with some other funds. Members can have control over the decisions of the fund, and finally, people may believe they can achieve better results when they can manage the fund themselves, compared with the poorer returns on investment achieved from some other larger funds. Again, this is debatable.

The Australian Taxation Office is increasing its compliance activities due to the growth of the SMSF sector in Australia in recent years.

ASIC are also vigilant as there are many spruikers taking advantage of people. There is also a prevalence of individuals and companies providing advice when they are not entitled nor permitted to.

What is an SMSF?

A self-managed super fund (SMSF) is a fund that must have fewer than five members. The members are generally involved in the management and the investment decision making of the fund. The members are required to be either individual trustees or directors of a corporate trustee of an SMSF. Lenders however may have their own policies on requirements of who is a trustee. Often it must be a corporate trustee. The amount a person needs to have in superannuation to make it worthwhile is also open for interpretation. From a lender's point of view, some lenders want to see $250k. Your financial planner can discuss what is right for you, or even if you should consider setting one up.

What are a few of the advantages and disadvantages of holding property in an SMSF?

It must be remembered at all times that with whatever advantages there may be in holding property in an SMSF structure, members are obliged to understand and follow the very strict regulatory regime in place and comply with the SIS Act (Superannuation Industry (Supervision Act) and the superannuation industry regulations.

If the SMSF does comply, 15% is the applicable tax rate in the accumulation phase; exceptions may apply, 0% on income and capital gains in the pension phase, with superannuation and death benefits receiving concessional tax treatment. If your SMSF fails to comply, and bear in mind ignorance is no defence, then the tax rate is 46.5%. Asset protection may be another consideration.

Disadvantages of holding a property in an SMSF are numerous; one main reason is the fact that investment earnings may not be accessed by the members until they have established a condition of release or retirement as provided under the sole purpose test. The biggest drawback I see is that you cannot access the equity in one property to use toward another property — it is permanently trapped until the property is sold; it simply cannot be used to cross-securitize the purchase of another property.

General expenses: accounting fees, audit fees, actuarial cost, and compliance costs.

Property expenses: real estate agent fees, depreciation, council and water rates, building write-off, and interest expenses borrowed.

Some specific SIS Act requirements

Sole Purpose test

The SMSF sole purpose is to provide retirement benefits to members. Trustees must consider whether purchasing property within their SMSF will satisfy the sole purpose test. One of the main issues that an SMSF auditor would look at when he or she audits a superannuation fund is whether transactions satisfy the 'sole purpose test'. This may be breached if monies are used for some form of personal enjoyment.

Investment Strategy

Trustees of an SMSF are required to prepare an investment strategy at the beginning of each financial year to determine the investment risks of each asset class and the ability to meet the member's current entitlements. The trustees must consider, within their investment strategy, whether the acquisition and subsequent use of a property and the percentage of the fund's assets would incorporate the property within its investment strategy.

SMSFs and borrowing

An SMSF is unable to purchase property from a related party of the fund, unless it is funded by current member's benefits. An SMSF is however, permitted to acquire property from a related party where the property is a real business property (commercial property or business purposes.)

An SMSF may be able to acquire a property if the property is completed, or 'off the plan'. Improvements being done on the purchased property would be a breach. The SMSF trust deed must allow the fund to borrow. Bear in mind that recently one of the mortgage insurers and some lenders are not comfortable with you purchasing a property being sold by a developer. The timing and creation of the bare trust and the purchase of the property is so important that documentation needs to be signed in the right order.

A loan under an SMSF is a non-recourse loan; trustees and members setting up this structure need to understand a non-recourse loan has restrictions in regards to other loans. If the structure is not right within an SMSF and is audited by an ASIC registered SMSF auditor, it will breach the regulations and the auditor has no choice but to issue a contravention report to the ATO (which would have the fund non-compliant regardless of its status.) The maximum loan against a property within a bare trust in the SMSF is 80%; you can refinance dollar for dollar.

Borrowing to purchase property within an SMSF is all about cash flow.

Some considerations to bear in mind may be:

- Sufficient cash funding to service the loan on the property
- Sufficient cash reserves to make repayments on the loan in case rental income is lost
- Trustees of the fund having adequate risk insurance, including income protection, to ensure that a superannuation contribution guarantee benefits is included.

Case Study

'As a registered SMSF auditor who is appointed by the trustee of the SMSF, the responsibility of the auditor is to express an opinion on the financial and SIS compliance report based on the audit of the SMSF fund. The audit is conducted independently based on an express opinion to the trustee. The financial report is prepared by the trustees of the fund, for distribution to the members, for the purpose of fulfilling the trustee's financial reporting requirements under the SMSFs governing rules and regulatory requirements.

'Issues that an auditor encounters when auditing SMSFs is whether older SMSF trust deeds have been updated to take up changes to legislation that is 'limited recourse borrowing arrangements'. The auditor must also make sure that financial and compliance reporting requirements have been adhered to, for example:

- *Bank accounts not going into negative over the period of the financial year*
- *Member's contribution caps for both concessional and non-concessional have been received and banked during the financial year*
- *Income and expenditure transactions has been imputed correctly*

- *Trust deeds have been updated especially to allow 'limited recourse borrowing arrangement'*
- *Investment strategy updated annually*
- *Trustee representation letter to the registered SMSF auditor need to be updated annually*
- *Process of purchasing property via the borrowing arrangements have been complied with*
- *Current 30 June market valuations on all asset class to fulfil members current benefits*
- *Member benefits have been complied with especially those in both accumulation and pension phase to determine the exempt pension income status*
- *Minimum annual pension amounts are calculated.'*

— John Couroyannis, ASIC Registered SMSF Auditor

When people want to set-up and invest in property within an SMSF, they need to understand the necessary decision making and be aware of the rules and regulations.

Follow this link to view my interview with Andrew Burgan, a mortgage broker specialising in lending for property in Self-Managed Super Funds.

http://www.austpag.com.au/premium-content

Chapter 10

Financial Freedom

'Nothing comes from doing nothing.'
— **William Shakespeare**

I have a quick question for you to ponder. It's the most important question you could ever ask yourself.

If we were connecting two years from today, and you were looking back over those years, **what would need to happen for you to feel really happy with your life?**

Take a moment to really consider that question.

Imagine it's two years in the future and you're looking *back* to today:

- What progress would you like to have made for you to feel really happy with your life?
- What would need to have happened? I mean, for you to be really happy.
- What would need to have happened in your life financially?
- What amount of money would you like to have invested?
- What would your income be?
- What about your health and appearance?
- Would you like to be slimmer? Fitter?

And let us not forget your relationships — including your relationship with yourself.

Would you like to have unconditional love and self-acceptance for yourself and everything you are?

You can really get into the 'picture' of your ideal future. You can:

See it.

Smell it.

Touch it.

Be swept away by it. Allow it to fill your consciousness.

It's a **great feeling** *'trying on'* your **new** life, isn't it?

Do you know why?

Because your **new** life is available to you **as soon as you start releasing all of your unconscious limitations** — doubts, fear, worry, struggle, resistance, etc. — that stand in the way of 'where' you are and 'where' you want to be.

Now, imagine you are now retired, you are very happy, and you have your family around you; you have more than $5 million in assets and a passive income of over $8000 per month? Your house is paid off; your car is paid off; some of your investment properties are paid off; you have $20,000 cash in an account to use; you are happy and have a smile on your face.

You are on a cruise; relaxing and enjoying it with your wife, your family, and friends. You provided this opportunity by the fruit of your labour, your foresight, and your investments. Isn't it a picture you can see yourself in?

176

All you have to do is release your unconscious limiting beliefs. I know you can certainly do it.

What is Happiness?

Happiness means different things to different people. I often ask someone what is happiness for him or her? They need to create happiness in their lives, and often they stop, think and don't know the answer. The big question is: how can we pursue happiness when we are not even sure what it is? So, what is it that we want to attract, what do we want to be, and what do we want to do with our life? Let's look at some qualities that can bring aspects of happiness into our life.

Most people that have productive lives and are filled with happiness have a sense of optimism despite the many failures in their life. Why is that so?

This is because these people tend to treat failure as a way of learning or changing their perspective, and are able to handle the same issue in a different way or to be able to move on. The learning they experienced results in an attitude of gratitude, appreciation, and value for what they already have. These people have an optimistic attitude and find their happiness by looking at the positives — they are grateful for the learning. This is in contrast with those who, instead of learning, are continually complaining about what they do not have, and often talk about their past. Past is history, and that's one thing you don't want to dwell on if you are to move forward.

Many a times we find that we remember the past in some distorted ways and we long and dream for situations that never were; so instead of creating our happiness in the present and in the future we turn towards a misconception of what life may have been like and idolize it into something that it never was or could have been. To make matters worse, we can dwell on the issue by holding onto this image that we built in our heads and live in that myth. In pursuit of happiness, we need to release the past. This may not be easy for some people, and it may not happen in a day. The good news is that it is possible to release the past and have a clear vision of your future and move on.

We are all human and we need good friends, loving family, and supportive friends and colleagues to bring happiness to those moments when we have fallen into a slump, and to share our lives in good times as well. It is vital to have people in our lives that care, and it takes energy and effort to keep those relationships in working order.

Often sadness creeps into our lives when we start to compare our relationships with others, and start to think that our relationships are not as good and begin to feel uneasy and inferior. However, it is important to remember that no two relationships are alike. Whether it's a friendship or a marriage, your relationship with each person needs to grow naturally, and caringly. This will flourish and benefit both of you and bring the happiness you desire.

We all need to be aware that when we have good relationships we can have happiness. Relationships are important; no one can exist on their own, as we need fuel to keep us alive. If we do not nurture and look after these relationships they will die. Perhaps many people are fooling themselves when they claim and believe that they are happy living their lives in isolation. They often call it their 'world', in their own heads and space: no one to worry about, no one to fight with, and no one to bother them. And the question is: how long can they be happy on their own? Research and studies show loneliness increases the mortality rate. And not many people will admit to it, but they are lonely because they believe they are too busy to worry about being lonely. Are they really being honest with themselves, or are they just fooling themselves?

There *is* a recipe for happiness and often we believe happiness will come from external situations, like our material wealth, and relationships. The truth is that our relationships with others and our relationship with ourselves are what bring a true contentment and happiness — one that does not exist in the materialistic wealth world. This is encouraging and empowering because when we know this, we have control of our own future and how we nurture others and ourselves.

There is no room for making excuses as to why we cannot move on and put all kinds of limitations on ourselves. We now have an ability to move on so that we can no longer become stuck and sabotage our lives. It is impossible to pursue happiness and move forward, or be able to grab any opportunities, when one is living a life of excuses and self-sabotage.

Whenever opportunities are offered to them, they have many reasons why they cannot do it. Or they make excuses that it was some other person's fault that they missed the opportunity.

If people continue to stay in that mindset, it is very difficult for them to achieve their goal in life or do what they really want to do.

If this applies to you, I need to tell you that you can now leave the negative — self sabotage mindset, bad attitudes, and negative beliefs behind and you can transform your life. You can create a more positive outlook and actually build new neurological pathways in your brain. And this means you can move forward physically, mentally, and spiritually and achieve what you really want (and always wanted) to do.

The following case study is of Pearl Yeo; a dear friend and a valuable contributor to this book. Pearl's story is told in her own words.

179

Case Study

'When I was young, I had a relatively good income and a fantastic lifestyle, with a modest share portfolio and a small savings. And life was free and fun.

'When I turned thirty I woke up with a shock. Looking back over those years, I had lots of fun and then suddenly I realised that I had not saved for my retirement. Yes, retirement seemed so far away at that age, however now that I am in my mid sixties it just seems like yesterday. What I did at the age of thirty was to estimate what I would need financially at retirement, and then I worked backwards to what I would need to start implementing from that day forward. I remember that in the beginning it looked like a wish list and seemed an impossible task at the time, but as I worked through the plan over the years it was not that difficult, and I did not have to make many sacrifices.

'I love my travel and in those days when my parents were alive, I would fly from Melbourne to Singapore just to visit them over the weekends. I loved eating out then with my friends and had a few favourite restaurants and I called them my "second kitchen". I still went to the theatre, musicals, and live concerts. I had sufficient funds to entertain and hold parties and I decided I just could not imagine giving all these up in my retirement, and so these "fun and good times" had to fit into my financial plan as well.

'My worst fear then was to imagine going to a restaurant, looking at the menu and saying to myself: I cannot afford to have this particular dish, or that desert, and so on! It would be traumatic if I could not have my favourite dishes, or I was going to be living in a less than preferred lifestyle in my old age. That is not on. I was determined that I would not go backwards in life by spending my future. To me, that was not a good picture.

'Both my partner, Athol, and I live off our passive income from some shares and mainly properties.

'My mother would say to me "cash is king". If you have money in your old age you will have many "friends", and everyone will want to know you and help you. However, if you do not have money when you are old, you will have to suffer in silence because no one will want to know you or care for you. That is ironic but truthful, is it not? Looking back now, at some of the people I know, I recognise how true this is. Their children don't even want to visit them now in their old age. I find this rather sad and feel sorry for them. However, you now know you have a choice and knowledge to create your own life.
— **Pearl Yeo**

So in working backwards and knowing what you want and need in your retirement, it is easier to establish a plan of action. When you are still young and working, it is easy to leverage on your assets; in particular, real estate or property. However, it is essential not to over stretch yourself because you still need to have a life and investments. You will build your wealth and yet be financially comfortable, allowing your tenants to help you pay the mortgage.

Many people tend to assume that if they work hard and save money then one day they will end up wealthy. This is wishful thinking. With this mindset, they are more likely to end up with some modest but useful savings, and unlikely to be wealthy. Many people are rather 'risk adverse' and they invest only in a term deposit (if anything.) Interestingly, these people are the ones who said they 'live a simple life and don't need much'. And yet, they do not take holiday breaks or go away for relaxation with friends and family. And they do not want to eat out — of course, there is nothing wrong with not eating out.

Research shows, that not many people are thriving. They are not fulfilled in their lives, nor excited about the future. To tap into the workings of human motivation requires a new mindset, a new skill-set, and a new habit — and it can takes years.

The following are the basic principles myself and other successful people have adopted towards creating a comfortable retirement which allows for travel, enjoyment of a better lifestyle, fun, and doing the things that better enrich our lives and the lives of others.

Of course you want to be rich, and you are entitled to have financial freedom, good health, happiness, and be able to spend your time and money in whatever way you want in your retirement. You could retire earlier and be happier, particularly when you have applied the basic rules.

The first step is to understand the basic rules of creating wealth

1. The time value of money concept
2. Savings and the power of compound interest
3. Invest in yourself and cash generating assets
4. Knowing your new commodity is not your labour, it's your ideas

Understand the time value of money concept

The key to financial prosperity is realizing the potential value of every dollar that you have in your hands and to think of cash as seed money — you can either eat it (spend it) or invest it (sow it).

In finance there is the concept that one dollar today is more valuable than one dollar a year from now. The reason for this is two-fold:

- First, a dollar will probably buy less goods and services in the future due to the destructive force of inflation.
- Second, if you have the dollar in your hands today, you can invest it and earn a return in the form of dividends, interest, or capital appreciation.

Savings and the power of compound interest

Savings

Frequently new investors ask how much should they be saving for investment. The question may at first appear to be straightforward, however, the answer is not so straightforward because it depends on many factors. For example, it depends on the age of the investor, their income, the risk profile, their lifestyle, and so on. And it depends on how much money and passive income they want to receive in their retirement. And we show you how to work all that out.

History shows that investing in a good profitable business and property are the best ways to generate income and grow your money. Therefore it is essential to save money so you have more money to invest.

It is essential to understand the difference between good debts and bad debts.

- Good debts are those that will grow in value over time. For example: house and property historically doubles in value in ten years if you purchase in the right area and the right type of property.
- Bad debts are those that depreciate in value from day one. For example: credit card debts, car, borrowed money for holidays, etc.

With a few notable exceptions such as good debts, debt is a form of bondage — a disease that enslaves the borrower. Therefore you need to recognize that bad debt is a habit that must be broken.

Knowing what bad debts are, the next step in building your wealth is to develop a plan to pay down high interest credit card debt. The credit card debt is probably the highest interest charged by any institutions.

Being free of bad debts and owing nothing

Imagine how your life would be without owing anything. You would own your car, own your house, you would have paid for your education, and you would be proud that you did it all yourself.

Like what you see? If you want to be financially free you will make it a priority to eliminate your debt quickly. However, say what you like, you need to seek a caring accountant who understands tax and investments to help you structure so that you can maximise your return. Remember: there are good debts and bad debts, and it is okay to have some debts, as long as you have positively geared investments in your retirement.

The Power of Compound Interest

Compound interest is interest paid on principal, and previously earned interest (or accrued interest.) Which means you can grow your principal faster.

Money is nothing more than a piece of paper with the image of a long-dead person on it. It is your understanding of the power of money and the value it represents that creates wealth.

Once you understand the power and value of money it hasn't got a hold over you because you know it is derived from your relationship with it; you suddenly become free from the constant pressures and stress of worrying about it. This is because you learn how to appreciate money: you know its value, you know what it can do for you and you know how to manage it. If you do not know how to manage your money, money will control you.

In particular, you will put money away for ten, fifteen, or twenty years and not keep constantly worrying how much there is. Instead, you simply make sure that you consistently and regularly contribute to the savings to increase the pile of money for your future. You will reach a point where you have a neat amount that is sufficient to invest. In that way you reduce your stress of thinking you never have enough money.

When you commit to saving money, you may notice yourself falling into the trap of spending an extra $5 here or there because you think, 'It's not that much. I'll never miss it.' However, this is a huge mistake, and you soon appreciate why such small amounts are very significant when you apply the time value of money principle and the power of compound interest.

Remember not to disregard small savings or small amounts as they will grow for you over time.

Invest in yourself and cash generating assets

Centuries of research and real life experience have proven that business ownership, property investments, and shares are the best asset classes on an inflation-adjusted basis. Historically the property value is said to double every ten years and is considered a stable investment if you buy right (i.e. buying property is about location, location, location — commonly, the right type of property in the right location.)

And yet, you cannot begin to invest unless you have cash left over at the end of every month, which means you need to save. With a positive cash flow property you still need cash for unforeseen circumstances, or any times between tenants.

With a saving habit, you will have cash to invest. When you invest in cash generating assets –such as buying an investment property — you have your tenant paying off your mortgage. When you buy shares with dividends that provide a reasonable return, you can reinvest the dividends to further help you to build your wealth. This will be less stressful because you will always have funds coming into your bank accounts, providing greater liquidity and flexibility, particularly in building your wealth when you are young resulting in cash flow in your retirement.

Shares are mentioned here in the context of it being a useful tool. A tool to be used by reinvesting dividends, to grow money, then — when you have sufficient capital — you could sell some of the shares as 'seed capital' for investing into property. You can later use the properties as leverage for the next property.

In order to create and build wealth it is crucial that you understand basic accounting, economics, and finance. You can either enrol yourself in a short course or do self-study. The initial cost for the training may seem huge at the time, however the knowledge you gain can make a large difference to your income, because you learn and understand the principles of accounting and how to manage your money wisely. The initial outlay for your education is repaid many times over during the years of your investment life.

For example, with the proper training in accounting, economics, and finance, you learn the best ways of investing in shares over time by knowing the dollar cost average over a diversified group of shares or a low-cost index fund. You learn that by spreading purchases over time, as well as reinvesting the dividends; your money buys more shares with a lower average price.

Think of it this way. If you spend $1000 to buy a 'gadget' for the home it may not make a lot of sense when you can sell it for only 5% or less at a garage sale. However, if you spend the same money to buy an old coffee vending machine, for example, and place it in a busy office where people are going to be putting money into it every day to purchase a cup of coffee, it will not only retain its value (because you can always sell the machine as a going venture in the future) and it has also provided you with cash income over those years. It is like putting coins into your bank.

Say what you like, no one can learn investing skills quickly without help. It may be necessary whilst you are educating yourself to seek advice or services of some experts if you already have the funds and are ready to invest. This is particularly vital if you are time poor. I sincerely believe that you must feel comfortable with the service provider you select because he or she is the person whom you will be working with. You must feel and believe you can trust that someone, and they must have integrity and have your interest at heart. There are many 'sharks' in the market place, and one needs to weed them out. You do not have time to waste with 'sharks'. This way you will learn a lot more about investments: where and what to buy to meet your requirements and own agenda. This way you can start your investment earlier and not waste your time and money.

Remember, no two people have the same needs and wants, and there is **no** one template that will suit everyone. At the end of the day only you, and you alone, will know what you want and what your requirements are.

Knowing your new commodity is not your labor, it's your ideas

Many people believe that they need to work hard to be wealthy. This is not the case nowadays because of technology. Many wealthy people started their own business from ideas they had, and it is no different these days. It is believed by many that it takes 'guts', 'courage', and 'perception' to set up your own business, especially when you do not know if it is going to work for you; giving up a regular pay cheque for an uncertain future is daunting. However, you have a choice, and if the opportunity is there, you can always start your business part time, initially, until the business income can replace and give you more than your regular pay cheque.

Successful, wealthy people are not held back by negative, limiting beliefs. They are often positive in thinking and attitude, and believe in themselves. They have a 'can do' outlook. Nothing is too difficult for them — they will give it a go. They believe in abundance and believe that their ideas will work for them. They also learn from their mistakes, and pick themselves up, and don't beat themselves down. Wealthy people have a mindset that recognises opportunities around them and leverage off these to create more income.

In comparison, people with negative money mindsets often experience poor results.

They struggle to pay bills, and often get caught up in the drama of when are they getting the next pay cheque, and (as a result) are always waiting for the next payday. They fear debt and often believe they do not deserve better jobs. They cannot see opportunities and will turn down opportunities because they believe it is 'too easy' and, therefore, 'cannot be for real'. The 'why me' syndrome so often ends in dead-end jobs and these people need not have to face a bleak future. This is because such attitude is not cast in stone; they can change if they want to.

So you do not want to go into your own business, that's fine too. You have ideas you can also invest in shares and properties. Many people have also become wealthy through their investments in properties or shares (and most likely both.) Why not let your money work for you for a change, instead of always working for your money? This is what will happen when you start investing in your ideas, either in a business, in shares or properties, or in all of the above.

As we get older, many people yearn for the 'perfect day' in their retirement. How do you live a perfect day, day after day after day? Isn't that what everyone wants?

One exercise you can do is to imagine that we have only a few days left to live and imagine what you would like to do in the last few days if money is no object. Then create a bucket list. This can be a rather entertaining and fun exercise. The reality is that even if you end up with a perfect day, and if you do it day after day, it will become boring and it's a routine.

At the end of the day we need to wake up to reality and face the fact that to be wealthy and successful we need to earn money; we need to save, and we need to invest to grow our capital and create income. What we need is to have ideas; we need to believe in ourselves; be committed to our ideas; use our savings to explore and learn from any mistakes instead of blaming them on someone or something?

Ideas breed more ideas, and the more you are able to tap into your inner mind, the clearer you will see. You will notice that you have become more positive when you start to change. You can see the opportunities, and will have more ideas, and will know how to access more funds for investments, etc.

No two people will have the same strategy — it may be similar, but not the same. Your future is in your hands and you need to own it. Be responsible for it so that you can enjoy the fruit of your labour, just as you intended it to be.

Life's strategy should not be a standard template. You and only you know what you want in your life and what future you seek. Do not allow anyone to talk you into a stereotype future, as this is your life. Take control. Own it, and take responsibility, as your future is in your

189

hands. Don't look back and regret because now you know you have other options.

In conclusion, remember this: once you are able to tap into your inner mind, you will know how to leverage your mind — you will never find yourself in an 'impossible' situation. This is because your mind will always be able to 'see solutions' that others cannot.

If you are reading this, it is because you know you are ready to embrace your 'new life' *and* **it is time for you to start your journey for transformation** to be a happier, wealthier, and more successful **you**. This is your life and you have helped to create it the way you always intended it to be. No one knows it better than **you**. So start your journey now.

This section has been provided to help people to possibly move forward in life and not get trapped by procrastinating and self-sabotage. Counteract negative thoughts of 'cannot' by switching your mindset to 'yes I can', and be able to take positive action to move forward.

Now you know everything is possible and you can do it.

'Come to the edge, he said. They said: We are afraid. Come to the edge, he said. They came, he pushed them ... and they flew ...'
— Guillaume Apollinaire

Team Working for YOU ... BONUS TIP

There are people with knowledge and people that lack knowledge. Having knowledge is not enough. Having access to knowledge and using that knowledge is key.

Landlord Insurance and Building Insurance provider

The cost of insurance can range from $220 per annum upwards, and is governed by the inclusions. Building insurance is always required and many lenders would like to see a copy of this, as well as the amount you have insured the building for. Prices that include landlord insurance range from $550 pa upwards. If you have purchased in Queensland, post the floods, there are many areas where it costs over $2000 (and in some cases it is impossible to obtain insurance at all.)

Quantity Surveyor

Get their name from the Bill of Quantities. In a construction project the labour and materials need to be assessed, accounted for, and itemised. The benefits of this are for valuation, but for investors it is primarily for depreciation schedules (taxation purposes). They prepare a document that the Australian Tax Office (ATO) will recognise as acceptable for tax deductions.

Property Advisory/Advocate/Mentor

As defined in the earlier chapters.

Broker

Refer to the previous section discussing this.

Accountant

Make sure your accountant has a personality. They should be friendly, and engaging, and have initiative. Even more importantly, ensure that they specialise in investment property, or at least have adequate knowledge.

Conveyancer

Make sure they can provide advice.

Check out my interview with Joseph Rose from Rose Lawyers.

http://www.austpag.com.au/premium-content

Property Manager

Refer to the previous section discussing this.

Building Inspector

Refer to the previous section discussing this.

> *'The law of diminishing intent says: "the longer you want to do*
> *something you should do now, the greater the odds that*
> *you will never actually do it."'*
> — **Frank Clark**

Insurances

I recommend you talk to an insurance provider/financial planner as you start growing a property portfolio. There are a number of insurances worth considering, based on your individual circumstances: life, income protection, trauma, and total and permanent disability insurances. Consider also talking to your lender about mortgage repayment insurance.

There are a few main insurances you should have for investment property: one is building insurance. If there is body corporate involved (normally always with units, apartments, and sometimes with townhouses) then the yearly body corporate fee includes building insurance. You must get landlord protection insurance in all cases. This insurance covers you for a number of different things, but can vary in the amount it covers you for. Major features include:

- Theft by the tenants
- Legal liability
- Accidental or malicious damage cause by the tenants
- Injury sustained by the tenant and guests — uninvited or invited
- Loss of rent due to tenant hardship, denial of access by tenant, death of tenant, default, broken leases.

Good Strategy

- Investing smart — have a plan and seek the right advice from someone representing the buyer; not the seller
- Replication — repeat the process to purchase more properties

- Balanced portfolio — having cash flow and capital growth properties
- Progress drawdown — during the construction phase of a dwelling, normally a house, each stage completed by the builder will result in the purchaser being invoiced for the amount attributed to that phase. This is always pre-determined by having a fixed-price contract
- Fixed-price contract — the building contract (which is based on what is being built and included in the building itself, and the price you pay for this) is fixed at an agreed amount, therefore protecting the buyer and, also, the builder.

Summary

I have intended this book to be educational in nature. Far too many people do not invest enough for the future for all sorts of reasons.

They don't know where to go or they are afraid. There are many things that are important to consider when investing in property and I have attempted to cover most of them. The most important being trying to protect you from property marketing companies by providing you with a solution that is an emerging market in Australia: property advice.

With investing in property through self-managed super funds, I believe ASIC are under pressure to work toward regulating the property market on all fronts. The model I use to help my clients is very likely the industry benchmark of how things should be (and hopefully will be.)

Often before you seek help from others you first need to help yourself, and hopefully the information in the relevant chapters in this book has worked toward achieving that.

We are on this planet and are living this life to *live*, not to work. The belief I have only recently instilled in my life is: I work to live; I do not live to work. You will rarely ever get rich working for someone else. Goals in life cannot be achieved working for someone else alone. You must take charge of your future. Your employer does not care about your future. If you do not care about your future then there is no hope for a future for you.

My mission is to help as many people as possible deal with someone who represents the buyer not the seller. My goal is to give back to the greater community — of which we are all a part, nationally and globally — by helping one person at a time. I want to share my knowledge and help you implement action toward your own better future.

Potential investors continue to be misled by many property marketing firms and spruikers to buy the wrong property, which culminates in failure to adequately plan, without the proper knowledge and the right advice. I believe that failing to act, and getting the right advice, is akin to failing to act on achieving the best possible future financial security for you and your family.

We have a six-step program you can follow to create wealth through property in a lower risk way, with less impact on your lifestyle and pocket, and I can show you how.

Visit the wealth builder blueprint http://www.austpag.com.au/ wealth-builder.html

I thank you for reading. The fact you have read this means you should be well prepared to move closer to achieving your goals, desires, ambitions, and dreams.

'*Andrew was introduced to me via my broker; as a young and inexperienced investor he provided me with options as to how best to approach properly investment. He understood my situation and what I wanted to gain out of my investment and used his contacts to both source potential property areas and present research for multiple areas. He went through each of his research areas in detail and then provided an introduction with a sales agent who had property in the area I found the best value in based on the research. After this Andrew was amazing as he was a valued resource for me to talk to while I purchased my property. I used his experience to help talk through my concerns and things of which I didn't understand as I was an inexperienced property investor, this was above and beyond what was expected of him to do. He was a valued unbiased resource and I was glad that I engaged with him first before my purchase and grateful that he was available for me to talk to all the way through my sales process.*'
—**Gautham R**

'*We have just engaged Andrew to research a couple of suburbs for us and source a new property. My wife and I wanted someone who was not aligned with any one Developer or Marketing company. Andrew Crossley was perfect. They first looked at our needs and goals before sourcing a property. A refreshing change from the spruikers out there who just want to flog their stock: Andrew does not sell stock and we loved the fact he was not incentivised to offer one project more than another*'.
— **Mark and Sarah D**

'*We found Andrew to be an excellent mentor, explained everything to us clearly in easy terms for us to understand. He was always available for us to ask questions, explain from his experience what he would do, responding in a timely manner. Nothing was too much trouble for him. Andrew was introduced to my wife and I by our broker. In no time at all, he was able find and secure an investment property that suited our needs perfectly adding to our portfolio*'.
— **Richard N**

FREE BONUS GIFT
TOWARDS MY SERVICES

AUSTRALIAN PROPERTY
ADVISORY GROUP
Answering your property investment needs

$375 Gift Card

This card provides credit toward the standard fee. This credit is non-transferable and non-redeemable for cash, it may only be used toward one of our property services offered. One card per client.

Contact Me

Enquire about my coaching program and other services in locating existing properties, new properties and providing advice.

Facebook: www.facebook.com/austpag

Twitter: www.twitter.com/CrossleyAndrew

Email: andrew@australianpropertyadvisorygroup.com.au

Website: www.australianpropertyadvisorygroup.com.au

http://www.austpag.com.au

Glossary

Development stages

Developers, who have carved up paddocks and acres of land into smaller blocks of land, will drip feed or release these for sale in stages to the public. This is to maintain pressure on prices. It allows the developer to increase the price of the next land release — often at $5000 or more than the previous stage of blocks. Each stage may have dozens and dozens of blocks. This is a way of controlling supply of the land to the market, and therefore protecting the prices in the area from reducing.

Display Home

A dwelling built with all of the possible upgrades and luxuries, and open for the public to walk through. It is used as a sales tool to sell similar style properties. It also provides people with ideas, thus giving them the incentive to spend more money on upgrades and additions. They can be purchased by investors, and sometimes come with two-year rent guarantees.

Equity

Most people do not use their equity wisely. Equity is the value of your property, less the debt you have against it. Ways to grow your equity could include doing some improvements on your property, and then getting it valued by a lender. Focus on reducing your loan on your home before reducing the loan against your investment property. You can make fortnightly repayments. The benefit of this is that you are not allowing the interest to capitalise on a large repayment. Interest capitalises daily, so if you pay fortnightly you reduce the interest being capitalised as much.

Infill opportunity

In a suburb where there is little to no more land where there is a block of land surrounded by houses, it is this block that may be able to be subdivided or built on. This is often achievable by knocking down the current dwelling as, generally, there are not many vacant blocks of land surrounded by houses on all sides. Of course, if there were many vacant blocks of land surrounded by houses, building on the land may not be worthwhile, due to a higher supply of these versus demand. As a result less money may be made.

Leverage

Using the lender's or another entity's money to make money/build wealth. Using other people's money to make money.

Spec Property

Occasionally builders build a few of these houses as a representation of what they can do, but it is not necessarily a display home.

Resources

http://www.moyak.com/papers/small-business-statistics.html

http://www.dynamicbusiness.com.au/news/did-you-know-80-of-businesses-dont-fail-2072011.html

Begin it now, Susan Hayward

Rich Dad Poor Dad, Robert Kiyosaki

Sorting out the good, the bad and the downright ugly of investment property advice, Terry Ryder

PIAA (www.PIAA.asn.au)

Forrester Cohen Services

Printed in Australia
AUOW01n1257140618
299010AU00004B/10